J. R Ramsay, Andrew John Ramsay

The Forest Light

And Other Poems

J. R Ramsay, Andrew John Ramsay

The Forest Light
And Other Poems

ISBN/EAN: 9783744659208

Printed in Europe, USA, Canada, Australia, Japan

Cover: Foto ©Thomas Meinert / pixelio.de

More available books at **www.hansebooks.com**

WIN-ON-AH :

OR

THE FOREST LIGHT,

AND

OTHER POEMS.

WIN-ON-AH :

OR

THE FOREST LIGHT,

AND

OTHER POEMS.

BY

J. R. RAMSAY.

———— • ————

TORONTO:

ADAM, STEVENSON & CO.,

BOOKSELLERS AND IMPORTERS.

1869.

TO

W. ORMISTON, D. D.,

This Volume is respectfully

Dedicated by the

AUTHOR.

CONTENTS.

CONTENTS.

WIN-ON-AH—AND OTHER POEMS.

Preamble.

GENTLE Reader, should the critic
  Think it worth his while to ask you
Whence this second publication ?
You will please to kindly answer,
Wherefore should it be avoided ?
Every man's imagination
Round some recreation lingers;
And, unless his mind is evil,
Let him follow his best feelings.
If with Livingstone thou wanderest,
Or in search of Sir John Franklin
Thou dost voyage; or dig ditches
For a living; or carve letters
Out of blocks for little children,
That their fancies may be filled with
Ample feasts outspread by learning,
Do thou do so : mayest thou prosper
In thy labour, it is worthy,—
If no duty is neglected.
If on fire with scenes majestic
Thou wouldst sketch, with brush and easel,
Lone Niagara's awful grandeur,
In the morning, noon or moonlight,
When bedecked in winter's jewels
Or enzoned by June's florescence,
Till thy soul is winged with beauty,
These are things to be commended.

2

If thy mind inclines to enter
In the fertile fields of fancy,
And thou sendest invitations
To congenial friends to join thee,
Why shouldst thou be asked to scribble
An apologetic preface ?
Should the oriole, or robin,
Or the grey wren give a reason
For their songs among the blossoms ?
Reason's not man's highest talent.
There are sacred facts for which we
Cannot give the why or wherefore.
If thou dost dislike the dew-drop;
Or the sunshine; or the storm-shade;
Or gay birds; or blushing rose-buds,
Pending from their leafy tendrils,
Soft in oriental lintels,
Vermil, green, or saffron tinted;
Or dost shun the lively laughter
Of the innocence of childhood,
When their glee is full upon them:
Go thy way—we part with pleasure—
We would not for all that's lovely
Harbor such a heartless critic.

But, if all these things delight thee;
If thou givest the cup of kindness
To the little one that's thirsty;
If thy daily toil is honest,
And thy mind is in thy labour,
And thy motive is improvement;
Yea, if beauty, truth and goodness
Form the motto of thy mission,
We will join our wills together,
And rejoice in mutual meaning,
In the fellowship of freedom,
Which, when found, is so refreshing.

Win-on-ah—The Forest Light.

On the eve of the Long Woods Battle, Tecumseh_desired his daughter Winonah to watch, from a hill near the battle field, for the return of his adopted son, Kumshaka, a white youth, who had been to the Sioux for promised assistance. Had Kumshaka not proved a traitor, the strife might not have ended in Tecumseh's death.

THE sun retired behind the hill:
  Slowly the glowing globe grew still,
Bathed in strange hues; a purple haze
Half moonlit, met the orient gaze.
Far as our mortal view could gain
Admission through the azure plain,
Evening a soft suffusion spread,
  A holy mournfulness on high,
A heavenly beauty overhead,
Such as the brows of Seraphs shed
  When harping in the upper sky.

So, silently, Win-on-ah came
To view her father's field of fame:
Thereon her brothers from the west,
Prepared for victory, or rest.

Her form was such as fancy sees
In grand ideal destinies.
Her eyes possessed that living light
Which kindles memory, as night
Is brightened by the dawn—a ray
Whose influence cannot pass away.
But words are worthless to express
The lofty light of loveliness.

Beside the Thames this youthful queen
Stood gazing on the sullen scene.
Among the shade, along the shore,
Her people held the mirth of war:

With menace fierce, and action wild,
That host the tedious night beguiled.
The scalp-lock, jasper-headed spear,
And eagle plumes waved weirdly there.
In forest aisles afar around,
Bright watchfires scorched the ferny ground,
And flecked the boles, and formed a breeze
Which swayed the sombre cedar trees;
They lit the waves that lurked below,
And gave the clouds a gloomy glow.
Forests on either hand arose;
Behind, the flood; before, their foes.
Each ancient chief, in daring bold,
Gave samples of the deeds of old.
Tecumseh spake: "The hunting ground,
Beyond the rolling thunder sound,
Is opened by the Manitou
To those who dare the deeds we do.
Our fathers' spirits, from the sky,
Demand revenge before we die:
Appease them! let the foe expire,
Like snow by flame—ere morning fire
The wand'ring cloud o'er Huron's wave,
Give every murderer a grave.
Who dares not die? who fears to give
This life, forever blest to live?
The white man shall pollute the graves
And cheat the children of such braves!
For deeds of guilt and faith betrayed,
Their sunshine shall be full of shade.
The black hawk from his cloud will come,
To see our wrath the foe consume;
And wheeling fearless round the sky,
Proclaim our country's victory.
The eagle on the withered tree,
     That overlooks the watery waves,
Has folded up his wings to see
     Our gathering for to-morrow's graves."

And when the misty morning broke,
They met as lightning meets the oak.
The Mohawk's war-whoop, wild and clear,
Was welcome as a word of cheer:
As fast the flinty arrows flew,
Each on its deadly errand true.
Above, abroad, anear, afar,
Arose the cruel crash of war—
The speedy stroke, the sudden yell—
As foe grasped foe and dying fell.

As wan leaves scattered by the wind,
As fear forsakes an angry mind,
As sand before the sudden breeze,
As waves upon the windy seas,
So were the long delaying foes
Dispersed before Tecumseh's blows;
So came his comrades in their wrath,
To fill the foul demands of death.

Win-on-ah saw her father's doom;
And yet Kumshaka had not come.
Why tarried he? the moon had past
His promise, waning to the west.

She watched in secret by the rock,
Feeling within her heart the shock.
Dim in the gloom of life undone,
With all her future scarce begun;
Then vanished, like a falling star,
On vengeance' ebon wings afar.

On Erie's shore there was a feast,
    And he, her truant choice, was there,
Receiving to his perjured breast
    A form whose smile he should not share.

* Win-on-ah by the water side,
Beheld him with his newer bride.

WIN-ON-AH—THE FOREST LIGHT.

The maple groves, where Autumn came,
Were all aglow, agleam, aflame.
By azure brooks the sumac stood,
And tinged them with the hues of blood—
Meet emblem of the mood within
Her heart, made hateful by his sin.

She gathered up her strength with all
Grief's subtle subterfuge and gall;
And smiled deceitful o'er distress,
As wormwood blooms in bitterness.
Soft were her steady words, and slow,
As moonless streams in midnight flow,
When falls the spotted ashen leaf;
But in her accent was no grief:

"Light of the changing cloud, this day
Hath fixed our nation's destiny.
There was no rider for thy horse,
Among our deathward-driven force.
We waited long, and did not know
What kept the arrow from thy bow.
Thy brethren battled by the hills,
Oppressed, but brave beneath their ills.
Our chief hath forded the dark stream:
His eyes upon the future beam!
How oft, amid the storm of war,
They turned and looked for thee afar;
Nor thought this idleness could be
Fit recompense for fame to thee.
Where is the color of thy cheek?
Has any come thy life to seek?
Think not that I am here to claim
The life that stains my father's name!
Go to thy race, whose greater light
Can screen whatever is not right;
Tell them Tecumseh's child can save
The wretch who filled her father's grave."

The Haunted House.

(A MEDLEY.)

"A jolly place in times of old,
But something ails it now."—WORDSWORTH.

OUR life resembles a deserted dwelling :
    The heart's an emblem of a haunted hall.
What will be from the first there's no foretelling :
    But disappointment happens unto all.

One summer morning, early in the season,
    Before the meadow hay was fit to mow,
I sauntered forth without an aim or reason,
    But just to woo the blossoms where they grow.

Full were the woods of music, and the meadows,
    On either hand, low-waving in the breeze,
Were gaily over-flecked with lights and shadows ;
    And O could you have seen the orchard trees.

The fragrant blossoms of the wild strawberry
    Brought back the memory of bygone days,
Wherein I wandered with the maidens merry,
    Knee-deep in clover over breezy braes.

My pathway led me to an ancient mansion ;
    Forsaken, wherefore few remain to tell.
A river bounds this valley's green expansion
    Of loveliness, and sorrow here did dwell.

The cricket sings his ditty unmolested,
    Where lusty dancers held loud revelry ;
The oxen of their yokes have been divested,
    And all the harvesters have gone away.

Yet they have left their long-unused utensils
    Against the gate, just where the work was done.
'Tis thus the peasant's plow, the painter's pencils,
    The actor's robe, survive the fame they won.

'Twas built with tiers of stone in upward ranges,
    Embrowned and battered by the blasts of old,
Seeming to muse upon the many changes
    Within itself, where owls their pinions fold.

A massive house, by all, save years, forsaken;
    Like living eyes, lit by departing day,
The panes look, when by winds the blinds are shaken
    With sounds that warn the wanderer away.

The mullein and the burdock fill the garden,
    Their growth the gard'ner comes no more to mar;
They look like orphans who have lost their warden,
    Blooming unblamed, for their sole neighbors are—

A pair of antlers in an archway standing,
    A seat for rest at twilight on the lea,
A broken boat below the reedy landing,
    A rusty scythe upon an apple tree.

With this worn scythe some vanished hand did sever
    The purple clover from the fields of green;
Another reaper gave him rest forever,
    And many summers o'er his bed have been.

Perhaps he held his curious speculation,
    Political, how empires rise and fall:
Perhaps ambition filled his admiration,
    Or learning lured him to her lovely hall.

Or having—who has not?—dismissed for duty
    Some chosen inclination, with a sigh
Oft mused upon the evanescent beauty—
    Hope's symbol—fading in the evening sky.

Or when the horn—sweet music!—called to supper,
  He slowly came commenting, from the field,
On farming, and the quantity most proper
  In hay or wheat for hilly land to yield.

Here whirled the spinning-wheel, that pleasant hummer!
  And graceful girls, in youthful beauty fair,
Came down yon pathway to the stream in summer,
  To bathe, pick berries, or meet some one there.

On this old beech, half wasted by the weather,
  Two names are carved by some enamored youth,
Sighing the while he fashioned them together,
  And dreamed of endless tenderness and truth.

What happened them ?—What comes to all the living
  In whose fond hearts Joy strives with Pain ?--two foes
Like two fierce angels, one of whom is giving
    Sweet solace; one, a demon, dealing woes—

Who, being stern and sturdy in his essence,
  Soon baffles all the blessings of the best;
And tho' young love stands longest in his presence,
  Even love must vanish, vanquished like the rest.

With "harvest-home" this hall was often lighted,
  Dancing, and music, and the ample board
Made autumn cheerful, travellers benighted
  Found welcome here and went away restored.

Now mournful winds among abandoned chambers
  Resound the anthem of departed days,
Whose nights have come, like soot upon the embers
  By the old hearth, which never more will blaze.

The dancers are dispersed, the music ended,
  The laughter silent and the lovers gone,
With their sweet schemes, on which so much depended
  And we are following after one by one.
  2*

Yea, we are following, smiling as we suffer,
  Taking an active part in our own pain:
While far around the misty waves grow rougher,
  We fondly hope next morn will lull the main.

We crush the craving cry of the heart's famine,
  We hush the hurricane whose wreck is years,
We hide the corpse which pains us to examine,
  We close the tomb on hope, the empty biers

Move, like the solemn clouds above the azure,
  Darkening life's pleasant mornings in the glade,
They baffle all our arts to seize or measure
  Their mournful depths of loveliness or shade.

First they are tinted with the hues of heaven ;
  But, like our hopes, their transient tints decay ;
As we o'er life, they o'er the earth are driven,
  Our prospects die, their lustres pass away,

Leaving remembrance like a raven sitting
  High on a dying yew tree's loftiest limb,
Whose withered leaves, upon the tempest flitting,
  Bestrew the graves, whereon our eyes grow dim.

For who, of all predestined to inherit
  Life's dreary dower, ever did obtain
The peace, the holy longing of the spirit,
  Or even partly conquer human pain ?

Those joys which the regretful spirit pities,
  Because they went too swiftly to the tomb,
Are no less mournful than the mighty cities,
  Pompeii, Herculaneum, or Rome.

Ah, well ! though every life in shadow lingers,
  Though long ere death can raise his hand to count
Our blasted years upon his bony fingers,
  Hope's golden bowl lies broken at the fount;

Though swift and sure our early aims expire,
    As if 'twere fate's first purpose to destroy,
It may be by such crushings we acquire
    The wine of wisdom which comes not through joy.

So time to all repeats the painful story;
    The farewell sun reflects the heavenly hues;
From nights of frost the forest gathers glory,
    A glory which the suns to May refuse—

Even to this mild Canadian scene and season,
    Whose vales, voluptuous, dreamily repose
In ever-varying hues, for which sweet reason
    I love this land of beauty and of snows.

O lovely land !—surely it would be better
    If we, like thee, our nature did renew
With a pure zone, like June's green flowery fetter—
    O beautiful world ! bathed in thy dawn of dew.

I love through forest avenues to saunter,
    Dream on the hills and trace the winding shore,
Familiar to the footsteps of the hunter,
    The silent race who visit them no more.

I love the lowly flower by the river,
    The dawning, and the glory of the west,
The wintry winds which make the woodlands shiver
    Till drifts upheaved defy the furious blast.

There is a rapture in tempestuous weather,
    A sympathy with suffering, which thrills
When midnight mists around the mountains gather,
    And hoarse winds howl among the moaning hills.

And the strong pines into the storm extending,
    Bow down as with an offering to the dead,
A tribute to the tempest, softly sending
    Snow-plumes unto the summer's funeral bed.

And when the gorgeous verdure is decaying,
   Serene September, by the hills and swamps,
Reminds me of an Indian maid delaying,
   Last of her race, among deserted camps.

Beyond the distance of a westward river
   Her friends have gone forever past recall;
Death put their days like arrows in his quiver,
   Fast as the showers of sanguine foliage fall

From blushing boughs that smile in silent slumber,
   Tinged like a cloud at rest on twilight air,
Or a great golden harp whose heavenly number
   Is hushed, because the harper is at prayer.

By vague tradition vagrant ghosts have haunted
   This house for years—its only owners now;
And many men have heard at midnight chanted,
   Most plaintive songs, and mournful, uttered low.

'Tis said, by doubters, that this sound increases
   When rude winds rub the branches of a tree
Against the shingles—such a foolish thesis
   Has no foundation—ghosts the neighbors see.

I put much stress on many a ghostly story,
   And relish every superstitious·tale;
It awes one to receive a guest from glory,
   A friend beloved it may be, out of bale.

Once too I had great faith in *human* nature—
   Dreams—which th' unfinished future did dispel;
For though I hate an unconfiding creature,
   My creed is changed, but why I cannot tell.

Because it would involve a long digression,
   And very likely make the reader mad;
'Tis best to shun the most remote expression
   Of aught would make a kindred spirit sad.

It is not wise to be too·sentimental,
   Although a fault that time will file away :
Our feelings are a sort of spiritual rental,
   A tax on talent which we all must pay.

But viewing man's estranged and false relation,
   The mental wealth we daily worse than waste,
Pains the full spirit for our crushed creation,
   Good yet, though by us all so oft defaced.

O Fiends might weep whene'er they fall to thinking
   Of all we might be and of what we are!
Instead of soaring we are suffering, sinking,
   Caught up in passion's whirlwinds—drifted far.

How carefully we plan to keep asunder
   Our inward anguish from this outward show!
It takes a life to rectify each blunder,
   Hence we excel in little else than woe.

Ah well! lest you perceive my theme's becoming
   Discursive, let us back into the trail :
My vagrant fancy is forever humming
   From theme to theme, as bees on flowers regale.

The neighbors say, when first these fields were settled,
   A man came from the land beyond the seas
To this blue stream—proud was this man, and titled,
   With riches, learning and long pedigrees.

He had an only daughter, says tradition,
   All beautiful as only daughters are
In fiction, with the sweetest disposition
   That ever crumpled linen anywhere.

'Twas care made her seem cold, and mute and clanish,
   Like pride, who lords o'er all except regret;
So friends went by as they are wont to vanish,
   When adverse angels all our aims upset.

O woman! thou art blamed for being blameless;
    Thy goodness is thy weakness, and thy snare:
O calumny, thy verdicts are so shameless
    That honor aches to curse thee, and make war

On slander, malice, and foul supposition;
    Those mean hell-raking hags whom I abhor,
Sneak round on Satan's most infernal mission,
    To mar the purity they know no more.

But musing on the melancholy kindness
    Of those young hearts which were too glad to meet,
Suffuses vision with a liquid blindness,
    Because their happiness was incomplete—

For she was fair and full of fond affection:
    The skies have scarce produced a purer love
Than heaved her snowy bosom's warm perfection,
    Filled her large eyes, or urged her feet to rove.

Her cheeks were like the light through rose leaves sifted,
    Expression pure, with hyacinthine hair;
But O her eyes—e'en Raphael, the gifted,
    Would fail to fix the feeling living there.

Fond was she of a walk, and the reflections
    Which come to lonely walks, by bush or shore:
There conscience seizes life's minute transactions,
    And daily promises to sin no more.

Not that she sinned, but it is beneficial
    To meditate betimes, and muse alone:
Church-prayers are pious, if not prejudicial,
    But thoughts grow pure when near great Nature's
        throne—

Yet, misconstrue me not, congenial nature!
    We own thy mighty power to conquer ill;
But in the mind of every human creature
    There is a void some loftier love must fill;

Which teaches that the Atheist, contending
    With Christian faith, has strewn vain whims abroad,
Forgetful that we're all forever blending
    Th' unfathomed facts of nature and of God;

Though reason, with the amplest information
    Earth gives, can scarcely prove what is to be
Beyond the awful verge of revelation,
    Which faith, through death, will shortly let us see—

So she turned rover by this moving river,
    Having few friends, and those illiterate;
But, what is strange to me, her guardian never
    Opposed her wandering from his garden gate!

Now who is this upon the moonlit water,
    Whose supple strength impels the swift canoe?
'Tis he from whom her father vainly brought her,
    Th' accepted one—O early love and true!

O early god of rapture and of roses,
    Dost thou remember by the western stile
Where first we met? may whosoe'er opposes
    Thy wondrous power "be choked in his own bile."

Yet we are sceptical about thy blindness;
    For right into the heart thy darts are driven,
Which taught me that a little damsel's kindness
    Can make this world seem a sublunar heaven.

'Twas in that season when the vales are vernal,
    A pleasant shower had left the evening skies
As glorious as the gate of the eternal,
    The pearly entrance into Paradise,

When Annah,—O that name of names! came sweetly
    To view the majesty by nature made,
And from that moment, though it passed so fleetly,
    I can see sunshine in the midst of shade.

Full was her beauty of that mystic power
  Which makes two hearts beat thrillingly or break;
Finding we could not live apart one hour
  We formed a paction for each other's sake—   •

But interfering with a maid's affection,
  Save to advise, is scarcely sensible;
Because she's bound to take her own direction
  Tho' death stands at the door and points to hell.

She went away with one who was her chosen:
  Her heart was breaking both to stay and leave:
It is so hard to have one's feelings frozen
  Between two foes, to both of whom we cleave.

She left a note upon the little table:
  Over her father dark misgivings came
Soon as he saw it; first he was unable
  To break the seal—who has not been the same?

Who has not stood without the strength to rally,
  To read the answer which some beauty wrote?
'Tis not unusual thus for me to dally
  With destiny enveloped in a note.

            "Father, thy mansion I have left,
              Gone from thy home away:
            'Twas hard to leave thee thus bereft,
              'Twas harder still to stay.
            I leave thee for my early friend—
              O wherefore do I live?
            One only hope my steps attend,
              Forgiveness—O, forgive."

This he re-read till reason almost left his
  Mind, too long torn by torture heretofore;
As an aged tree, by lightning lately cleft, is
  Found to have been long blighted at the core.

" He swore a prayer or two," he called for horses,
    He kicked the dogs, he made the servants run
On several different ways and various courses,
    But all in vain, the tender deed was done.

After some trying days of forest travel,
    At last they reached their lowly island home—
Time rolling on, as usual, to unravel
    Joy's few frail threads from griefs eternal loom.

Poor lived they, and unpardoned; for *position*
    Makes many parents mar their offspring's fate :
Years after this the bride obtained permission
    To find her father; but, alas ! too late.

Gone was he, gone the father ; and the lover,
    When she returned ; all, save her ghost, are gone:
It sometimes comes the graves to murmur over
    Of the unfriendly father and the son.

I often wander at the twilight hour
    Near this dim nook, but never stay at night.
They may not like to meet me in their bower,
    And so I leave, through reverence, not through fright.

'Tis gloaming now; great Sol leaves heaven's expansion ;
    Uncertain shades move eerie down the dell :
A pre-engagement urges my attention,
    So, for a little season, fare thee well.

The Shell.

One vernal morning, mild and clear,
Thé oriental atmosphere
Flamed golden, saving there and here :
   Clouds of pale crimson
Kindled a goodly dawn as e'er
    Wild birds sang hymns on.

As some great theme untold in rhyme,
So grandly Sol began to climb
His azure dome to measure time,
   High in mid-heaven :
All underneath his smile sublime
   Appeared forgiven.

That holiday, remembered well,
Not feeling fit in crowds to dwell,
Up, pensive to the mountain dell, .
   Lonely I sped ;
But finding in the street this shell
   Thus musing said :

To be where thou art is not good,
Commingling with the common mud ;
Thy hues, like roses in the bud,
   Blush there to be :
Once bathed in ocean's ample flood,
   The ancient sea.

The soft suffusion of thy face
Proclaims a sentimental grace :
That thou art greatly out of place
   Thy lot is proof—
'Tis thus with all the tuneful race,
    Neath heaven's blue roof.

Hadst thou to some green lane been taken,
Where from the foliage dews are shaken—
Winged harps by living hundreds waken
   Those dawns with glee—
Thy fate had been far less forsaken ;
    But *here*,—ah me!

Let not thy gentle heart be hurt
Because we meet among the dirt ;
If we are forced with filth to flirt,
   Not ours the wrong ;
It was not sent thee to pervert
    Thy wavy song.

Let me expunge this outward stain,
(It does not mingle with the grain)
That thou mayest murmur of the main ;
   What there befel :
O, could I take thee back again,
    And with thee dwell !

By what far island wert thou born ?
Did Neuha have thee for her horn ?
Did Montezuma's host forlorn,
   Sound their retreat
On thee, alas, that cruel morn,
    By Cortez beat ?

Can it be possible that she,
Who dwelt beside the Indian sea,
Virginia—gazing on that lea
   Which is her grave—
Ran down and from the tide took thee,
    Rejoiced to save ?

Thy murmured answer, mystic friend,
I cannot wholly comprehend;
Yet some things in our nature blend;
    A lurking gift,
Whose holy longings upward tend,
      Yet fail to lift.

Come to my dwelling in the garret,
What room is there I freely share it;
(A boon begrudged is minus merit
    And burns the hand)
There thou wilt find the great in spirit
      Of our loved land.

Serene among the muses shining
S. Moodie, Wilkins, P. S Vining,
Friend Haney, capable of refining
    Castalia's tank;
Souls for whose work fame's not designing
      Oblivion blank.

Shakspeare and Bunyan both are there;
Von Humboldt, with his hoary hair
Like thine own sea; and Burns, the rare
    First son of fame;
John Milton, mounting Jacob's stair,
      Blind unto blame.

Some who have long ago.departed,
Some by death's sickle lately thwarted,
Some who great schemes improving started,
    - And lost the way,
Some minus money, broken-hearted,
      Died waiting pay.

One struggled hard to help the needy,
Reclaim the sot, and clothe the seedy
Fit for the Universal free day
      Which will ensue;
But this huge world has grown so greedy
      What can one do?

All that we hope for does not happen.
Angels perverse (our deeds mis-shapen?)
Wrapt his high aims a shroud of crape in,
      Making them vain,
While he, sole mourner of fate's rapine,
      Stood bound by pain.

He was transported by a spell,
When beauty's glance of glory fell
On his fine spirit—there to dwell
      For ever more:
As from dim caves an ocean shell
      Heaved high on shore.

Bounding the lambs went o'er the leas,
Like foam upon the windy seas;
The growing leaves on lofty trees
      In dew stood glancing,
Waiting the music of the breeze
      To set them dancing.

But just as he began to dream
His world-regenerating theme,
Disgusting disappointment's stream,
      Above him rushed:
Where storms, contending, scowl or gleam
      His harp was hushed.

There was a time when men were proud
Along with him to be allowed:
E'en queenly beauty kindly bowed,
      (His hat ascending),
But once beneath misfortune's cloud,
      Behold the ending!

Still—(though we merit melancholy,
In common with man's fall and folly)
When adverse tempests, drifting lowly,
      Eclipse the skies ;•
Some Sabbath prospects, sweet and holy,
      Awake, arise.

We have a grand exhaustless store
Of large impracticable lore;
We can feel music long before
      The first note sounds;
Far off we hear stormed ocean roar,
      Lashing his bounds.

Sweeter to us the crickets sing
Than harps to hearts of harsher string:
Each flower's a very holy thing,
      In color dressed,
Like bands of angels entering
      The realms of rest.

We can afford to pity those
Who scorn a poet's joys and woes;
Their earthly fancy never flows
      From light supernal,
Where truth's millennial laurel grows
      In youth eternal.

Though we are blamed when not to blame,
By those who deem we sing for fame,
We know the right, yet suffer shame:
      Forced wrong by wrong,
E'en while we struggle to reclaim
      The erring throng.

Think not, dear friend, thy lot is hard,
Because by pain from peace debarred,
Maimed, menaced, mutilated, marred,
      Beyond a cure;
Great pains produce a great reward,
      If we are pure.

My fellow-sufferer in distress,
Fame's phantom beams would blast, not bless,
If we fail dumbly to express
      The light within,
The holy light of loveliness,
      Because of sin.

Lose not thy faith, look on heaven's scroll;
How grand the midnight orbits roll!
Think not the mind that has control
    Of such a scene,
Can stain its honor, or extol
    Aught that is mean.

Upon the time of trouble's spite
The muse can soar by second sight,
As through the embattled storms of night
    Bursts heaven's red ray,
Till earth is deluged with a light.
    Fairer than day.

So, bard of ocean and of time,
Come and commune in wordless rhyme,
About thy coral halls sublime,
    I do beseech;
Grant me some knowledge of that clime,
    Beyond the beach.

For o'er an ocean we must sail,
Soon as we quit this adverse vale:
We send, but no return of mail
    Comes from that coast:
It cannot be in death's dark gale
    That all are lost.

Love and Lucre.

Slow rises worth by poverty depressed.—JOHNSON.

O thou inexorable hag, 'twere bliss to curse thee.—HEAVYSEGE.

The children born of thee are sword and fire,
Red ruin, and the breaking up of laws.—TENNYSON.

Chill penury repressed their noble rage,
And froze the genial current of the soul.—GREY.

Money answereth all things.—SOLOMON.

NOW, while dark clouds roll heavily with rain,
  And yellow yarrow waves along the lane,
Let the tired team rest in the cosy shed—
The polished plough is in its russet bed—
While forests bow before the coming gale,
Here we will muse as fancy tints the stale,
The actual pageant passing day·by day,
The joys that perish and the pains which stay.
Sweet is that season when our spirits feel
The wordless peace—so painful to conceal ;
When every passing beauty claims the eye ;
And *one*, far more than all beneath the sky,
To whom we bow instinctive, offering her
The "firstlings" of the heart, nor once demur—
A time that comes to all—what tho' unknown
This goddess be, each throb attests her throne;
And woe be unto him, yea, more than woe,
As many a grief-grooved brow and tomb can show,
Whose offering is repulsed; the sky for him
Is leaden-hued henceforth, and cold and dim.
Autumnal tints dwell on the drooping trees
Through all the year; and darkness throngs the breeze
With that high, mournful, unresigned regret
Which follows, and defies us to forget.

That man is weak who thinks on his life's leaf
The fatal fang of some especial grief
Has fixed itself forever; yet we know
There are deep channels where few waters flow;
There are stern storms that howl alone at sea;
There are proud heart-pangs in prosperity;
There are green glades clothed in continual glooms;
There are high hills where sunshine seldom comes;
There are gay barks that never gain the shore;
There are grand souls sin-stained for evermore;
And many sigh, "Ah me! not mine, not mine!
'Tis hard to bear, but bitter to resign:
The lips may laugh and yet the bosom be
Sad as the shadows of Gethsemane."

O love! fond folly, influence undefined,
Unbounded king o'er all of human kind,
Few are the odds if thou art cursed or blest,
Thy road to ruin's shorter than to rest;
Thy joys are birth-day journeys to their grave,
Thy blisses bubbles on the breaking wave;
For love is suicide when hope is vain,
Compassion torture, and all pleasure pain.
O for a life uninfluenced by such things!
The outer story and the inner stings!

Still there are compensations: few but know
Some secret sources of delights that flow
Into the eager soul.   At times life's seas
Lie calm as mercy's smile, or charity's,
And thousands turn when their affection dies,
And chant this ditty to a wealthier prize:

O Lucre! thou enchanter, champion, chief,   ˂
God of the monarch, merchant, miser, thief,
Mankind succumb to thee; plebes, princes, priests,
Fools and philosophers flock to thy feasts.
Majestic power, to whom earth's Bacons bow;
For whom broad seas, even the grave, we plow:

3

There's not a monarch on this moving world
O'er whom so broad a banner is unfurled;
None have such faithful followers; who revere
Or hold their other gods so high, so dear!
Wisdom is weak, though large of heart and bold,
Unless her goodness is upheld by gold.
For liberal salaries learned men we find
Who mend the mouldy morals of the mind.
The great majority, when all is said,
Deem even meanness merit if well paid.
What urged the Spaniards hither? glory! yea,
And what is mortal glory minus pay?
What use is fame sans gold—whatever can
We do without its sanction and amen?

Mammon, to thee I dedicate my strain,
Sire of success, celestial and profane.
Once (blush O weakness) once I undertook
To write against thee an abusive book.
Thy pardon, if I said or sung a strain,
Or thought, which pierced thy mighty brow with pain:
'Twas envy, that foul prompter of crushed pride,
Which urged me to dethrone thee and deride.
Great Mammon, let us worship, let us bare
Our thoughts to thee, for thou art ruler there.
Six days we follow after thee, six days
And nights—except when Cupid claims our praise—
And on the seventh day demurely creep
Up to the house of the Most High, and sleep.

'Tis thine to marry empires; second son
Of Time, thou hast thy brethren all outrun;
E'en sable Death: obedient to thy sway,
His silent hounds release their shuddering prey;
For Gain can buy up Death, and coin control
The unknown voyage of the vanished soul.
And thou canst bind the lover to his bride
Or sever him forever from her side—
Since Venus married Mammon 'tis decreed

The god of wedlock is the god of greed.
Thou art the ballast in life's ship, and none
Can sail without thee; compass, keel and sun,
Our hearts rejoice in heaps of thee, and quaff
The wine of wealth, and all who win thee laugh.
There is no innate guilt in thee, O gold,
More than in eve's bright clouds which we behold
Rosy and beautiful, as they have rolled
Through all the unsung histories of old;
The fault's with us who falsely get or hold—
Thou'rt tinged by us, as water by a sieve,
Our passions tarnish even what we give;
And all thine ill comes through the lives we live.
Thy name is magic; necromancy dwells
Within thy coffers; all that most excels
Is at thy beck and bidding; matrons leave
Poor mates, and to thy favourite followers cleave.
What millions marry thee; thy smiles reclaim
The scraggy wryness of the wrinkled dame
Who bears thy ponderous purse; 'gainst thee what chance
For poor young beauty, with its glorious glance?
War's thy weird holocaust; he wantonly
Whets his red knife, and nations pass away,
Though empires watch the issue, still and stern,
Dreading the debt of Death, and angels mourn.
Beauty is bought by thee; the spirit's thirst
'Tis thine to satiate, e'en the best or worst.
How much we owe to thee; ingratitude
To call thee evil's root, thou root of good.
By thee the student passes on his course,
By thee the worthy rise from much that's worse.
We clothe ourselves by thee; our very blood
Is bought by thee at market with our food;
And since our brains are made of blood, and thought
Is born of brain, our minds by thee are bought.
'Tis wicked to deride thee: 'tis unbrave,
Because society's thy serving slave.
Thy cold avoidance of toil's nerve-strained strife
Has whetted many a suicidal knife,

Till Tophet's gates are jammed by those who stream
The road to ruin—
           Let us change the theme ;

Few riches cleave to ruin ; even song
Detests it, beauty dwells not in its throng.
Loose-jointed fear, and hollow-breasted care,
And disappointment mourn together there.

Boast not of sweet adversity and toil,
Ye who sit gorged aloft and share the spoil.
Your minds relaxed by ease, can never know
The want that weakens everything but woe.
I feel for all, but most for those I feel
Who loose this linch-pin out of Fortune's wheel.

O youth, ere yet to penury resigned,
Print Shakespeare's precept on thy plastic mind:
" Put money in thy purse," and it will be
A loadstone to entice prosperity ;
Join the majority, get gain, or thou
Wilt find misfortune through thy vitals plough.

The rock of Sisyphus refers to coin,
Be-deviled like the Galilean swine.
That things should not be thus we'll not deny,
But these facts' defamation we defy.
The dread, the burden, and the restless goad
Of Debt drags hosts down ruin's zig-zag road.

My curse upon thee, Poverty, my curse
Upon thy hide-bound, constipated purse !
Thy woes have withered millions, great and free,
By fierce, resistless, stern astringency.
Thy steps are blight and murrain; madness takes
The mildew of his spirit from thy aches.
Thou hast no reverence in thee, no respect
For feelings—none are prone to thy neglect.
Thou unabortive incubus of doom,
Hinnom's ambassador, and virtue's tomb.
How can domestic kindness gladden more

When thy gaunt wolves howl hungry at the door ?
Uunnumbered hosts, refusing to be slaves,
Ungrieved, unknelled, fill thy forgotten graves;
And millions mouldering now in lowly clay,
Have worn sad smiles to hide their dread decay.
The cruel smile of friends, who could not shun
Thy threadbare coat half-faded by the sun.
E'en he whose bosom burned with love to all,
Was forced to drink thy wormwood's withering gall:
He saw the dark gehenna spread before,
And struggled to return, but all is o'er.
Cold now, and prematurely paled in death,
The breast that never drew a debtless breath:
The human loves, the heaven descended muse,
The horned hands, the labour-hardened thews;
The broken hopes, great nature's lordliest friend !
Found in the grave at last grief's holy end.
O human love ! We know thee; thou art strong—
To Mammon's minions mightier powers belong.

I said, while standing near the scaffold high,
Of one crime-doomed, impenitent, to die:
" Hold, prize of Death; before too late unfold
What broke thy moral moorings from their hold ?"
"Stranger," he spake, "thy starting tears restrain,
Till I unroll my downward years again :
Short is the story, and my journey too ;
My term is full, the debt of nature due,
Which in a few brief moments must be paid,
For lack of lucre and those hopes that fade.
The substance of my solitary tale
Is often told in silence to the gale.
By my youth's home lived some kind friends, tho' poor :
The wind found many an entrance round their door ;
The sickly parents toiled by turns to gain
Some scanty nourishment to strengthen pain ;
Yet Peace, the Peace which poverty allows,
Was stinted round, and centered in that house.
There the clean poker leaned against the jamb,

There kindness mingled with connubial calm ;
The pine-knot flames played round the rustic room
At hide and seek among the gleeful gloom.
Joys they had seen—who cannot say the same ?
One child was theirs ; by her my sorrow came—
Pure, bashful, faithful, beautiful and free,
With all her fondest fancies turned to me.
'Tis wrong to name her here ; my spirits ache,
E'en at this ending hour, for her sad sake.
Suffice to say, a richer rival came,
And I am here a criminal in shame,
For troubles came, till in my spirit's storm
I cursed the folly that produced my form.
Punished with pain, pierced with more promised woe.
O, for her sake to shun th' abode below !
O, spare me from my memory ! O, save,
Or it will blast my soul beyond the grave !
The future's black, with ruin unresigned ;
But spare the past, I dare not look behind !"

Another instance : By a sylvan stream
Dwelt one whose fate it did a symbol seem ;
Fairer than day she was, or dewy dawn
Outspread by May upon a sunlit lawn ;
And he, her choice, had wealth in ships and cars;
And, seemingly, no clouds eclipse their stars—
But 'twas the same old tale of Whittier's lay :
"Maud Muller" in the meadow making hay,
Was left, because her dower was less than his
Who loved her—such this world's decision is—
Till down adversity's dark Malestrom driven,
They went to spend their honeymoon in Heaven.
Tho' oft in lucre, and in love no less,
The bitterest curse is coupled with success ;
Impetuous Passion, with a zealous zest,
Woos this wild solace to his woeful breast.
But this unto thy children do thou teach :
Be honest in thy dealings, each to each,
Make what thou canst by upright motives make,
And use it for some truth's celestial sake.

Tasso to Leonora.

THE suns of many years have set
   Since last we bade a long adieu.
I told thee I could ne'er forget,
   And what I told thee then is true.

The might of manhood seemed in vain,
   When forced thy fondness to forsake ;
When told we ne'er might meet again,
   I knew my heavy heart would break.

I said, how shall I let thee go ?
   How shall I set my spirit free ?
I know despair, but do not know
   How this great balefulness can be.

Tears are for tenderness to shed,
   But not when torn from such as thou :
My very destiny is dead,
   My faith forsakes the future now.

Through years of night my spirit bleeds
   With thought—soon conquered, were I free !
But memory with thy kindness feeds
   My solitary constancy.

I see thee in the dreams which flow
   Back through the baffled years of youth ;
Yet when I wake, alas ! my woe
   Exceeds the bitterness of truth.

The Bluebirds of Spring.

"And something earlier every year
The singing birds take wing."
J. R. LOWELL.

HAIL, singing symbol of the Spring !
   With all thy flowery train.
To every valley of our land
   We welcome thee again.

Come to the pine and maple tree,
   To groves of willow come ;
The buds are weary waiting thee
   To woo them into bloom.

Here is your very same snug nest,
   Built by the ancient barn,
Made soft with feathers from your breast,
   And tiny bits of yarn.

Fill up the little nest with love,
   And all its wants relieve
Among the twilight-tinted grove
   Slow-waving in the eve.

Fresh greenness and the fragrant flower
   Shall glorify the glade ;
And fruits abundantly will dower
   Thy sweet domestic trade.

When wintry tempests from the sky
   Frowned on our landscape lone,
We longed to see thy forms flit by
   As in the summers gone.

We longed to see the oriole here,
   The robin and the jay,
Fly through the firmament and cheer
   Our labour all the day.

And though remembrance of past mirth
  Will with thy songs return,
So many joys with thee have birth
  Remembrance shall not mourn.

Then welcome, symbol sweet of Spring,
  With thy congenial train ;
To every valley of our land
  We welcome thee again.

The Desert.

INTO the desert of my heart
  I sometimes gaze awhile,
Upon the ruins scattered there   .
  Of many a stately pile.

Lo, at the very gate of life
  A temple used to stand :
Its walls are crumbled into dust,
  Its dome is in the sand.

Its centre high was like unto
  The deep blue dome of day :
Bards in its halls of heavenly light,
  Were welcome guests alway.

Now not a living mark remains
  Of that vast mansion there :
The wind howls dreary o'er those plains
  Which formerly were fair.

Majestic friends who came and planned
  Improving schemes with me,
Some went into a far-off land ;
  Some went into the sea.

3*

You're none the worse for that.

To G. Roberts.

I SAW that wealthy fool drive by,
    With your beloved just now ;
But judging from her pensive eye,
    She will not break her vow ;
Yet should she, one sweet truth we know,
    Which peace can ne'er get at,
They who to grief's great college go
    Are none the worse for that.

I know your troubles—trod that way
    Since vanished sweet sixteen,
On many a sultry summer day,
    The plough's hard shaft between.
But reason—banishing false fears—
    Gave, when his conclave met,
The verdict of the vanished years,
    You're none the worse for that.

Most men have been by Cupid's flame
    Too deeply scorched to scoff ;
Yet it is best to have some aim
    To wear those feelings off.
The headlong impulse of the heart
    May plunge us in regret,
Till we would rather die than part—
    We're none the worse for that.

And you who think your lot is hard,
    And doubtless it is so—
Upon your memory print this card :
    The worthy meet most woe.

At life's great feast of pain partake
   Of what for all is set ;
Though your fond heart with anguish ache,
   You're none the worse for that.

You suffer not alone, nor I ;
   This autumn of hope's spring
Made the immortal Milton sigh,
   And Burns—how sweetly! sing :
In pain they saw the smoke upcurled
   From their dead joys, and yet,
The moral glory of the world
   Is none the worse for that.

Peace to their ashes, the great dead,
   Who never got their due !
Their feet o'er flinty pathways fled,
   Their works remain to you:
Their poor old sinewy hands all day
   Were tanned in labour's vat,
Building this beacon by the way,
   You're none the worse for that.

And we who are abused by man,
   (By woman much the same)
Captive in Cupid's very van,
   Unknown to human fame,
If half is true what sages say,
   A seal is on us set,
Whereon engraved we'll find some day,
   You're none the worse for that.

Visit of the Angels.

ONE Sabbath evening, from the land of light,
  A host of angels winged their earthward flight
Hither from far Valhalla's halls—they were
Weary of that repose which we prefer.
Vast worlds on worlds, inhabited and high,
Songful, surrounded them fast wheeling by.
As stars in Spring, so they in glorious robes,
Sang gleeful anthems with the choiring globes.
Then came a rushing sound among the shade;
And lo, this orb, our dwelling, onward swayed :
Through lurid gloominess its wastes appear,
Barren and sterile, bleak, austerely sere.
Huge thunder-splintered pinnacles and rocks
Frown on the ocean's unexhausted shocks,
Where every wave, heaved from its caverned source,
Clasped by the cloudy storm's tremendous force,
Exultant, surged along the scowling sky
Or back into their ebon caves did fly.
Tearful, though faultless, tremblingly they reach
The luneless loneness of the bloomless beach;
And lighting on a city-bounding hill,
With their white wings lit up earth's living ill.
Upon this scene they gazed, while time rolled back
Death's woful scroll, exposing what we lack,
From earliest records of Ambition's stress,
Down to the Present's boastful restlesness—
Full of the plagues which pain the little span,
The sensual downfall of degenerate man;
In pride or want, in avarice or strife,
In some dark form each man a foe to life ;
When contrite tears bedimmed their tender eyes,
Beholding whence our rapid ruins rise.
Time them assured that yet this living stream
Would turn, and move mild as a morning beam ;
And men be knit by love to bravely bear

Each adverse burden, and alternate share.
Not long they looked, not long before they knew
Their home was brighter far above the blue;
Compared to this, where they had lately been
Thrice happy was ; but trebly cursed this scene.
The climate of the upper sky is fair ;
'Tis Sabbath afternoon forever there.
The sun so dimly shines he sheds no shade
On any object ; all things are arrayed
In their own merit : mercy brightens some :
Wisdom awards an everlasting bloom.
Far thro' Valhalla's ante-mundane dome
Deep bells pealed praises and proclaimed them come.

———

On Seeing the Teeth of an Ichthyosaurus in Barnum's, Broadway, N. Y.

PERHAPS thou hast strayed where the Mastedon neighed
    With lordly Leviathans lone :
Or craunched the strong snake in the slime-oozing brake,
    By heat-heaving mountains of stone.
When morning scarce broke through Cimmerian smoke,
    And chaos unclaimed knew no sun :
That epoch of old, ere the star-choir extolled
    The uncursed creation well done.
Alas, that thy date, from Oblivion's strait,
    Is washed by the torrent of time :
For then we might know why earth welters in woe,
    With hells of unharvested crime.

O could the dark clouds which mortality shrouds
    Be wafted for ever away,
Our vision might count all that was since the fount
    Of the light we denominate day.

The Temple of Fame.

___

To my Father.

___

THE residence of Fame has been described
By Pope who from fount Helicon imbibed
Pure inspiration; freshened by those springs,
Buoyant and bold, he spread his skyward wings
On visionary voyages, and brought
Much wisdom, hived in ample cells of thought;
And when his thither flight from earth was done,
They crowned his head and called him Homer's son.

Beyond time's shore, upon a crystal hill
The structure stands; far from all earthly ill.
The turrets high are hid in glory's blaze,
Which fairer grows the farther up we gaze.
Broad are the walls, bound firmly with the lost
Egyptian glue, embayed with beryl, embossed—
Resembling fountains fretted o'er by frost.
Columns of polished porphyry engrained
With gold, the lofty balconies sustained:
Branched in Corinthian arches to uphold
Broad beams of beryl, and roofs of glass and gold,
Wherefrom vast domes heave into the eterne,
As ocean icebergs in the sunbeams burn.
The fleecy clouds effulgent, float and glow
Forever there, majestically slow.

There Shelley dwells, rapt in millennial dreams,
Pale moonlit radiance round his resting beams,
Angelic music lures him fondly nigh,
And fancy fills him with congenial joy.
While florid Sol suffuses all the west,
Moved by the scene he muses into rest.
But many more have gone, since Pope's release,
Into the temple of eternal peace.

There Burns, high priest of nature, prince of song,
Spreads his vast soul around, or joins the throng;
Or hand in hand with Highland Mary strays
By streams like Ayr o'er bonnie banks and braes.
Leave them by broomy heaths of fragrant shade,
Where milkwhite thorns wave fair, but never fade,
Above that modest crimson tipped flower,
Whose deathless lustre decked their trysting bower.
There all the peace this earth his heart denied,
With one who once was lost, is by his side.
She gazes on the bard, while far around
His songs extend to Fame's extremest bound,
Spread east and west, by trump and timbrel spread,
Soothe every soul, and cheer the cherished dead.
Harmonious hosts his daily steps pursue;
To tune their harps is all he has to do.

The Answer.

MY friend, I cannot take thy hand,
   And tell thee what will be :
The future is so dimly planned—
   Who can his fate foresee ?
But I more graves than thou have past,
   More epitaphs discerned,
And from the horoscopes they cast
   Some precepts haply learned.

We grasp at phantoms insecure,
   And grieve when they are gone:
The disappointments we endure
   Are oft from seeds we've sown.
We scatter flowers upon the stream,
   To see them whirl away,
Then sigh above the symbol of
   The joys which will not stay.

How oft we nurse within our hearts
   The fault we charge to fate,
Then seize the dram to soothe the darts
   Which conscience can create ;
But though we join the gambler's game,
   Or drink delirium's bowl,
There is an awful sense of shame
   Within a sensual soul.

No potion, powerful, of wine,
   No deep oblivious drink,
Can ever quench the gift divine,
   Th' immortal gift, to think.
According to the depths we go
   Down crime's degrading course,
While thought, reacting, brings us woe.
   Or withers with remorse.

   How lovely are the fresh green fields,
     Lit by the morning sun,
   When every dewy flower reveals
     The work in darkness done ;
   So from the shadows of distress
     We, too, may rise ere long,
   For sorrow is the warrior's dress,
     Which makes the wearer strong.

But there's a light we overlook,
   Or vaguely view in dreams—
As heavenly flames refracted crook
   Low in the reedy streams—
That light a holy life supplies,
   A bow when fortunes frown,
That dies not when the tempest dies,
   Nor with the sun goes down.

Brutality Triumphant.

THERE'S not a more repulsive truth,
    To those who love their race,
Than to review earth's rearward years
    Of glory or disgrace,
And find how oft mere brutal force
    All godlier gifts defile
To some abused uncertain power
    Less than a little while.

How oft the world has been laid waste
    By demons bad and brave,
Thrones, cities, empires, learning's halls
    Hurled blood-surged to the grave.
All shameful shapes of mingling crime
    Red history's pages smear,
From records most remote of time,
    E'en to the date most near.

'Twas ever so with those grand souls,
    Who strove to lift the load
Of ignorance and oppression's bonds
    From off the hosts they goad.
They strove to rear among mankind
    Truth's temples pure and high,
Those martyrs to their fellow-men
    Did desolately die.

Too late, too late, the laurel leaves
    For Tasso's brows were twined;
Spain starved her Homer, Scotia's bard
    Was to neglect consigned.
What kings enthroned have loved their kind
    Like the mild sons of song;
Yet who in ruin's arid realm,
    Received from men more wrong?

Great Daniel in the lions' den,
  Golgotha's cross and pains,
The persecuted Christian host,
  Columbus in his chains,
Galileo forced to veil the light
  Of truth's celestial beam;
What millions have neglected gone
  Down time's insatiate stream.

Yet earth's first nations, even now,
  Received with golden fame,
Yea, paid two splendid human shapes
  For deeds surpassing shame.
God's servant, too, and statesman learned,
  All eagerly stood by;
Each left his post while brutal force
  Was hailed triumphantly.

◄═✖═►

Dante to Beatrice.

NO song contains a tone of so much sweetness,
  However sweet, as thy persuasive voice,
No flower fresh from morning such completeness
  Of beauty as thine own, my only choice.
Nay, the most lofty loveliness of spirit,
  Made pure by prayer—too pure on earth to be—
E'en when high hopes were thine—is minus merit,
  And fades, eclipsed afar, compared to thee.

Beneath the lamplight of the sleeping city,
  In the pale moonlight of the pensive grove,
To all our trysts I sing the tender ditty,
  And make our paths familiar with my love.
But thou! alas, thou art not near to listen!
  Thou never more mayst hear my harp again,
Nor watch with me eve's opal dew-drop glisten,
  Nor list the nightingale's forlorn refrain.

But fancy often fills thy vacant places—
   Not vacant from my heart but from thy side—
And, as of yore, I gaze upon thy graces,   .
   Till woe, soon wakened, proves that fancy lied.
Yet willingly I welcome the delusion,
   I dare not say adieu, dear dreams, adieu!
My heart is torn too oft by truth's intrusion;
   So welcome dreams—O that those dreams were true.

The Glade where the Dandelions grew.

HOW often when weary with labour,
   The duty of man unto man,
   We open the gates of remembrance,
   Where infancy's rivulets ran.
     Even now, while the sun over Huron
   Gives evening a lovelier hue,
    The spirit of nature reminds me
Of the glade where the dandelions grew.

One beautiful morning in May-time,
   When birds were preparing for June,
Some red willows waved in the breezes,
   That rippled a little lagoon.
The sky was embellished with azure,
   With flowers the landscape, and dew;
We chose our companions and wandered
   To the glade where the dandelions grew.

The scene was celestially favored,
   It baffled art's exquisite touch—
Ye scarcely could fancy how Eden
   Surpassed it in loveliness much;
The ferns and the pearl-tinted lilies
   Bowed low by the waters of blue;
When she gave me her beauty forever
   In the glade where the dandelions grew.

Though pain after pain has distorted
  The heart that was happiest then,
I remember our mirth when we sported
  At hide and go seek in the glen:
The beautiful twilight of heaven
  Bade nature a blushing adieu,
Ere we came from the lake in the valley,
  The glade where the dandelions grew.

The cloud which arose on that eve
  Was the spray from adversity's wave,
But her tenderness made me believe
  In a heaven this side of the grave;
And so few are life's scenes of rejoicing,
  That fancy delights to review
The first of the fields that were fragrant—
  The glade where the dandelions grew.

I never returned to that valley;
  I never can go there again;
The change that came over the real
  Would make the remembrance a pain;
But often look back to its beauty,
  And sigh o'er the sweetness we knew
As we sat by the blackberry bushes,
  In the glade where the dandelions grew.

And you who have much speculation,
  Who struggle for bread or for gain,
Till the beautiful love of your boyhood
  Has almost forsaken your brain—
Even you have your moments romantic
  In the crowd and the counting-house too,
Some scene that is lovelier than lucre,
  Some glade where the dandelions grew.

The Lane.

AIR:—"*Just twenty years ago.*"

ONCE more I linger in the lane where we have often strolled,
I need not tell you which it is—you know the spot of old;
Those zigzag fences are the same, the meadows all as green,
And to a stranger passing by, no changes can be seen.

Upon the sward the snowny clothes are spread about to bleach;
From bending apple boughs the fruit is hanging most in reach;
On the old porch they've gathered some in the warm sun to dry;
And by the garden edge the pond is azure as the sky.

It is not many years ago—I wish that time had stayed—
Since, underneath this very tree, our promises were made;
Great was my joy to see the glance and sparkle of thine eye,
When first I told my preference, and gave the reason why.

Your voice I seem to hear again; I see you as before—
The very pattern of your dress—the bonnet which you wore;
But grievously reality dispels the vision dear,
As eagerly I look around, and find you are not here.

I know that men of lore may laugh to hear a lover say,
That nature's laws can change because a maiden's gone away;
But much I fear, against my hope, that more than this is true,
For something else is also changed—and dearest, is it you?

O, had we known, before we met, 'twould be so hard to part,
Surely we would have saved ourselves this aching at the heart.
Time and again I turn to go, as often stop to view
Those scenes which all the coming years can never more renew.

How soon hope's green and golden leaves begin to fade and fall!
At frosty dawn the birds repeat their mournful muster call;
I too must sing a sad farewell—not only to this scene,
Not only to the happy past, but all that might have been.

Sallust's Home in Pompeii.

BEHOLD, at Pompeii, in Sallust's home,
　The relics of an orgie in a tomb !
The bosom of a dancing girl is pressed
'Gainst his, the bony framer of a jest.
The unbaked bread was in the oven left,
And in the fruit the knife by which 'twas cleft ;
The supper table charred, the wine jars dry,
And those who came to dance remained to die.

It wounds our large assumption to survey
What folly death o'ercomes us at, what play !
The humble, and the men whom circumstance
Hath favoured—all are targets for death's lance—
All low alike at last ; and none can tell,
If this dust was a king, a clown, a belle.
What alchymist can take this brainless bone
And swear this bowed, this ached upon a throne !
Once this head's wit ran through the social room,
This bony cheek blushed beauty's bygone bloom.
O, could this skull—still eloquent in death,
For thought will rule beyond the bounds of breath—
Give us an index to th' immortal mind,
Of those who come to bless or curse mankind.

<hr/>

Lena Lee.

OUR active toils for good or bad
　Are rounded off by sleep ;
And every human heart was made
　To laugh, and love, and weep.
We laugh in life's young boundlessness,
　We love when hearts agree,
We weep to lose some gift of grace
　Like lovely Lena Lee.

There's not a power that girds the soul
  For great deeds or for hate,
That grasps with such supreme control
  The storm-driven helm of fate,
As beauty; if 'tis used for wrong,
  Woe unto future glee;
For few but feel some golden thong
  Like lovely Lena Lee.

Her lot is lowly, and her hands
  Are often tinged with toil;
Yet eager to undo the bands
  Of penury's cruel coil—
Oh, kindness greater is than kings!
  In virtue all agree;
Yet both are unpretending things,
  Like lovely Lena Lee.

The longest river's reedy race,
  The seasons rolling by,
The whitest cloud compelled through space,
  The wandering sun on high,
The wings of time, the orbs of night,
  The seraphim, sin free,
Find none in all their rounds of light
  Like lovely Lena Lee.

Her words are ever pure and true,
  For wisdom rules her mind;
Her eyes are of the loveliest hue
  'Tis possible to find;
And yet the little violet flower,
  Beneath a lonely tree,
Is not more modest in its power
  Than lovely Lena Lee.

The Hamilton Cemetery.

JUNE, 1867.

A LOVELY place of loneliness, the spot
    Whereon the warm sun lingers to illume
The residence of friends too soon forgot,
    While flowers symbolic spread unseen perfume.
Ye scarce could think that under all this bloom
    The worm is busy with the beautiful
Untroubled tenants of the tearless tomb;
    Feasting in fearful silence to annul
All that we dread to be, e'en death's celestial lull.

Lo! to the east outrolls a living sheen
    Of liquid azure, tinted from on high,
Mottled with moving sails, engirt with green;
    And far around the sunlit landscapes lie.
Here love's lost links and broken dreams defy
    The fondest bosom's yearning; westward, lo!
A very Paradise regales the eye; *
    And dimly distant, where the daybeams glow,
Far over Flambro' hills my childhood's rivers flow.

How oft in youth I watched thy wandering waves,
    Blue stream! and longed thine ending to explore.
Here thou hast led me to this land of graves—
    Drifting my hopes into this dim *no more*,
Where mystery sleeps on death's horizon shore
    Unroused by time—here the gay cricket sings
And beauties, with their followers, traverse o'er
    Green paths by flowery graves when Sabbath flings
    Soft floods of radiance round, from light's supernal
        springs.

---

* Cook's Paradise: so named after a young officer who came here on a hunting excursion, in an open boat from Niagara. On his return, being asked where he had been, he replied :—" In Paradise."

Again this green Canadian hill is clad
   In efflorescent leafy loveliness :
These wild birds sing as if they never had
   So many sunny praises to express.
O for the peace of Nature ! no distress
   Hath scarified her countenance, no pain
Corrodes her vital vigor—born to bless
     The homestead of the heart which thirsts in vain
     For any other home, save the celestial plain.

To meditate on beauty, to admire
   The wonderful in forests, by the shore,
In solitude, when twilight doth expire,
   Hath been a joy of joyousness, a lore ;
And if at times a face appeared, which wore—
   Or seemed to wear—an index to such love,
'Twas sweet to follow such ; but evermore
     Reality mine error did remove,
     So fancy roams afar where reason would not rove.

These grassy graves seem like the waves of fate,
   Forever anchored on this winsome strand.
Here bickerings end, with earthly doubt, and hate,
   With all our little schemes in trouble planned.
The mother led her first-born by the hand
   At early morn, then parted, weeping here,
Where summer smiles in slumber, lightly fanned
     By breezes from the upper atmosphere,
     Among these waving groves where war's green mounds
       appear.

4

To Anna.

WHEN first I saw thy loveliness,
    My heart took angel wings ;
And when I heard thee speak, I said,
    Surely a seraph sings ;
But when I clasped thy lily hand,
    And viewed thy radiant eyes,
I looked around confused to see
    If more had left the skies.

Song.

AMONG the vales a maiden dwells,
    The noblest of the living,—
O come and view her beauty, you
    Who deem my song deceiving.

I tell thee, friend, no art can blend
    The smile of such a creature ;
Her cheeks defy the rose's dye,
    As mind surpasses nature.

But come not near to interfere
    Between me and her splendor ;
For, if she wills, through all life's ills,
    Henceforth I shall defend her.

I'll get a cot in some sweet spot,
    Where nature smiles serenely,
For I would give a world to live
    A life with one so queenly.

June.

THE summer is coming, with honey bees humming,
  And hawthorn trees blooming in every green nook :
The wild birds are singing, for nature is bringing
  Fresh flowers up-springing, and blue to the brook.

Green forests are waving above the green paving,
  And gay clouds are having a dance in the sky ;
When weary with flowing they turn to the growing
  Bright flowers, bestowing fresh dews from on high.

But now a dim shower re-enters with power
  A porphyry tower of many strange hues ;
Formed chiefly of shady effulgences fady,
  A skyey arcadia, a home for the muse.

Then sweet smiling nature, with joy in each feature,
  Half dumb, like some creature subdued by surprise,
Looks up to the azure in evident pleasure,
  And takes the great treasure with tears in her eyes.

O Nature, how neatly thy garments befit thee !
  O summer, how sweetly thy coming can smile !
We know some fair creatures, with love-kindled features,
  But beauty like Nature's can never beguile.

The children are quitting their sports, for 'tis getting
  The hour of the flitting of birds into rest ;
And slily the lover goes stealthily over
  The fields of red clover, to one he loves best.

Hail, delicate greeting; such moments of meeting
  Are ever too fleeting, too happy to last !
Hail reason and science, in every appliance,
  But love's first alliance is purest and best.

For somehow its promise no sooner goes from us
  Than clouds overcome us to vanish no more,
Except when some vision with vivid precision,
  Returns, in derision, the joys that are o'er

Then welcome, young smiler, youth's pleasant beguiler,
  Ere blight, the despoiler, shall wither thy bloom ;
A little while longer, when passion grows stronger,
  The great ironmonger called duty will come.

When reading of folly, of passion unholy,
  Or dark melancholy that lives in lost loves,
I said : I will master this foolish disaster ;—
  But my heart beats faster than reason approves.

The Wild Canadian Whip-Poor-Will.

MY friends are those who love to hear
    The songs that fill the atmosphere,
When under evening's dawning star
Familiar landmarks fade afar ;
And vesper hears from every hill
The Wild Canadian Whip-poor-will.

'Tis sweet to hear an evening bell,
With all the feelings that upswell,
When fancy pictures many a scene
Of joy that was, or might have been,
Since first we heard, beside the mill,
The Wild Canadian Whip-poor-will.

But now that we are far away,
That ditty brings a memory
Of what no song, or martial strain,
May ever reproduce again:
So memory loves to cherish still
The Wild Canadian Whip-poor-will,

Again I view the vernal thorn,
Which blossomed by the old log barn;
And hear that chorus break the hush
Of twilight in the sugar bush,
Whose dim old arbors echo still
The Wild Canadian Whip-poor-will.

As human minstrels often sigh
For things unutterably high,
As all men mourn some loss of light,
And chant their dirges in the night,
So, haply, disappointments chill
The Wild Canadian Whip-poor-will.

Persuade me not the nightingale
Relates a more alluring tale
Among Italia's laurels old,
Where centuries of ruins mould ;
For we are free as on each hill
The Wild Canadian Whip-poor-will.

Song.

AIR.—*Afton Water.*

HIGH over West Flambro the fleecy clouds flow,
The rivers rejoice in the valleys below ;
But there is a beauty far fairer to see—
It's O to belong to a being like thee.

Behold this bright landscape, so lately the zone
Of summer, 'twill shortly be winter's white throne;
But thou canst make summer wherever we be,
It's O to belong to a being like thee.

We'll steal out and stroll where the shore-bended stream
Leaps up in the light of the living moonbeam,
To the bloom-tinted tryst of the old willow tree;
It's O to be loved by a beauty like thee.

I long to be near thee when weary with toil,
I long to delay in the light of thy smile,
As a sailor looks out for his home from the sea;
It's O to belong to a beauty like thee.

⊷≉⊶

A Dirge.

To ELLEN.

MY sister, when I look upon the vanished,
    The voiceless past where all my hopes lie dead,
I feel like one from his own kindred banished,
    For some dark crime, to a far country fled.

There is no crime—yet a great shadow hovers,
    Like mists which keep the mariner from shore—
Hiding the isles of peace which hope discovers
    In early life, from me forever more.

So life's unanchored bark goes drifting vainly,
    Where rude winds veer, and sullen waves roll high;
And all my efforts have this ending mainly,
    Warming to life the worm which will not die.

My aim was once to aid whom fortune slighted,
  My bent to benefit the trouble-crushed;
The faith of those who trusted me is blighted;
  Whom I could teach have for my folly blushed.

Hushed is the voice which there is no forgetting,
  Cold the kind hand which might have led the way
Into the silent land of suns unsetting—
  Leaving a weary wanderer astray.

Where was the use, O heart, in all thy hoping?
  The bowl is broken, and the fountain dry—
Poor blinded Cyclops, round his cavern groping
  For some lost door, is happier than I.

Yet blame not one who has no right or title
  To hope or happiness, here or to come :
Whose lofty longings end in the recital
  Of dreary dirges o'er a dreadful doom.

<hr/>

Forewarnings.

SAY is it superstitious fear,
  If we believe, from Hades drear,
Some evil influence night and day
Disturbs our better destiny?
Who with a finite mind can seize
The soul's intangibilities?
There often moves across our path
The misty blasts of coming scath ;
Whose drear forewarnings do diffuse
A shade o'er all we loathe to loose ;
And we are troubled long before
Misfortune enters at the door.

E'en to the innocent they come,
Those whisperings of the spirit's doom— .
Dim phantoms, bearing pleasure's pall,
Most terribly distinct withal.
· Dark omens settle on the soul,
    Defying reason's piercing beam,
In mental mists, like clouds that roll
    Their shadows round an unseen stream,
To warn us as we move away
Among the things of yesterday.

The Dominion of Canada.

BY every green valley, dark forest and lake,
    The sword in thy service we will not forsake:
The song of our hearths shall be Freedom and thee;
A land has no home till its people are free.

Behold the oppressors of Africa's child !
Their gains are polluted, their glory defiled,
Their country's a shambles from centre to sea ;
A land has no home till its people are free.

They say our green valleys to others belong ;
We have not a Court and we have not a Song—
Best so (though 'tis false) than with bondmen to be ;
A land has no home till its people are free.

We're free from their servile transgression and stain,
Who barter their daughters like cattle for gain :
The laugh of a slave is a terrible glee !
A land has no home till its people are free.

We love thee, my country, with all that is thine,
Thy valleys of beauty, thy mountains of pine,
Because thou art free from thy lakes to the sea—
A land has no home till its people are free.

Arise, some great singer! repeat it to earth,
All nations are blest by the progress of worth;
And others may follow as soon as they see
A land has no home till its people are free.

A Reverie.

THIS night the winds are gathering storms,
   To sift them over hill and home:
Fancy is full of phantom forms.
    And this dim room.

The backlog has grown black with cold:
   A thicker shade is on the floor:
Deeper and deeper drifts are rolled
    Against the door.

What scene is this my fancy sees,
   Which makes my listening pulses thrill?
Rest, rapid fancy, if you please,
    Rest and be still.

'Tis but this fading pine-knot flame
   Hath made that other flame revive;
Yet something syllabled her name,
    As I do live.

There was an old house in a grove,
   Sheltered by storms, whene'er they blew.
There dwelt a damsel all did love,
    And I did too.

Doubtful and shy I went to woo,
   When life was young, yet longed to learn;
And when up to the door I drew,
    Wished to return.
    4*

Some blossoms in the breezes swung
  Beneath the mossy cottage gable:
As loud the little crickets sung
    As they were able.

Pleased she appeared—soft ringlets played
  Round changing cheeks by blushes stained:
Anon the old folks bedward strayed,
    But we remained.

We spoke of various things, and strove
  To hide what each desired to know—
Such is the evasiveness of love
    In its first glow.

A jar of flowers was on the jamb,
  Upon the mantlepiece a clock;
She sat in sweet domestic calm,
    Mending her frock.

'Twas harvest time, and hemlock boughs
  Bedecked the hearth where fire had been;
Some books were there, and all the house
    Was very clean.

O'er clover fields the moon-beams gleamed,
  The old dog howled out on the hill ;
Yet, to my heart the whole house seemed
    Uncommon still.

But soon acquaintance grew apace,
  In gossip of the neighbourhood ;
The hours began a rapid race,
    By joy pursued.

Time's wheel hath certainly some flaw,
  It rolls so fast when all is well ;
Perhaps 'tis owing to some law
    El-lip-tical.

To a Rev. Friend.

HIS brow appears like eloquence enthroned.
   Who is so learned as he to make our clay
Lovely as earth by joyful June enzoned ?
   He sweeps all creeds from immortality,
As night is banished by the god of day,
   Till scoffing sceptics bow abashed to heaven,
Or sink like waves hurled from high rocks in spray
Down to the depths whence they have vainly striven,
Whilst multitudes revere the gifts so grandly given.

O for a mind like his to comprehend
   The hidden and the high—of holiness
Earth's noblest sample : eager to befriend
   The needy in the season of distress.
The soul's Shekinah in Doubt's wilderness,
   Where Pain's dark paths grow denser hour by hour,
And every step is down,—who would not bless
The hand that lifts and leads, with such kind power,
From out the arid waste where death dwells to devour?

From the prose of Carlyle.

TO A. G. RAMSAY.

YOU wake to work, and do not shirk
   What duty bids you do:
The strength of life is in the strife,
   Tho' dreadful storms ensue.

Improve the mind, and be resigned
   To what you *cannot* mend,
For time misspent brings discontent
   And shapes a dreadful end.

The insects sing upon the wing
    An hour, then disappear:
They do their share : not any are
    In vain by God sent here.

The little flower, the sunny hour,
    The storms that blacken heaven,
The hopes that bless, or bring distress
    Are all in kindness given.

How many a year this mundane sphere
    Has waited for your lot;
One life on earth will stamp your worth,
    So disappoint it not.

Then guide, altho' fate's sullen floe
    Drives fierce against hope's prow;
A time of bloom will surely come
    If we but labour now.

There is no state, nor low nor great,
    From which we cannot rise,
If we but feel that human weal
    Is sacred to our eyes.

The strongest mind that moves mankind
    Might some weak idiot be,
But for the power the present hour
    Confers on you and me.

Be great, if thou wouldst preach or plough;
    A day's work is a prayer :
Receive to give, and thou'lt receive
    A more abundant share.

Paul says there's more, when life is o'er,
    Of wages coming due,
If we will brave temptation's wave
    To win the good and true.

To a Lady.

Madam, I do, as is my duty,
Honour the shadow of your shoe tie.—HUDIBRAS.

YOU are much like the maid who delighted my fancy,
    When beauty first kindled the delicate joy,—
She came to our barn-yard one evening with Nancy,
    (Our milk-maid was Nancy when I was a boy.)

Her cheeks wore the shell-blush, her forehead like lilies,
    Her step put the fawn of the forest to shame,
Her voice was as glad as the brook in the valleys;
    But praise of such beauty seems foolish as blame.

Bewildered I blushed before such a beholder,
    Having been at a logging bee down on our farm:
A fork full of hay dangled over my shoulder,
    An armful of provender under my arm.

Upturned were my pants and my hat was in tatters,
    Slouched over a countenance sooty and dim:
The hat was a felt one, so long from the hatter's
    But little was left save the ribbon and rim.

She saw how it was, and did kindly endeavour
    To banish the pain of my boyish distress:
Then came the sweet truth which will linger forever,
    That women of sense never slight a poor dress.

So sneer not at rags, for experience taught me
    That sensitive worth is so easily hurt;
And honour in patches this parable brought me:
    The meanest of men often wear the best shirt.

And there are so few that make goodness a duty,
    My heart may be broken but cannot forget;
For she left round remembrance a halo of beauty,
    Like light round a cloud when the sun is just set.

Caliph Omar.

ONCE when the Caliph Omar came
  To council with his men of fame,
Two Arabs leading, bound, a third,
Approached requesting to be heard:

" Brothers we are who bring our cause—
A father killed—(he kept thy laws)—
Whilst walking in the garden air;
This culprit came and slew him there,
Then fled, we followed far, and caught,
And him for retribution brought."

"Answer," the Caliph Omar said:
The young man calmly raised his head—
The beauty of his countenance
Was his most eloquent defence.
" My judge, what they have told is true,
And more, which shall be known to you.
I am a Bedouin, and the land
From whence I came is desert sand:
Up to your city walls there came
Our peaceful camel, young and tame:
He browsed the branches of a tree,
And this an old man chanced to see;
He hurled a stone against its head
And crushed my little playmate dead.
Enraged I raised the self-same stone,
Which from my hand was swiftly thrown:
The blow was deadly, and I sought
Safety in flight, but here am brought."

" Thou hast confessed thy crime," replied
The Caliph, "let our laws decide:
Retaliation is the pain
From him whose father thou hast slain."

"My doom is come," he did reply;
"But, one more deed before I die.
My dying father in my care
Left a young brother; and the share
Of shekels which falls unto him
Are hidden in the desert dim:
Low buried in a place unknown
To any save myself alone.
But if you cause my sudden death
Before I get him his bequeath,
Commander of the faithful, you
Must answer to the prophet true.
Grant me three days; but do not fear."

"And who will be your surety here?"

Alazon, Omar's prophet, said:
"My life is thine, in this youth's stead:
Although a stranger, I will be
The captive Bedouin's guarantee."

Three suns o'er the red desert rolled,
And yet the stranger came not back;
The plaintiffs asked Alazon bold
For blood—their vengence would not slack;
This his companions did deny;
But Omar said, "Our seer must die;
If at the sinking of the sun
The youth delays, his days are done."

Lo, at that moment up he came
To answer honor's dreadful claim.
"The heat hath hindred me, but I
Am here, father—must I die?"

"Commander of the faithful," said
Alazon, "I have stood his stead,

Inspired to confidence and grace
By beauty in a stranger's face:
No longer say there is nor worth,
Nor truth, nor honor upon earth."

All were astonished; and the two
Who came to slay, their suit withdrew,
Clasping his hand; while Omar gave
Full pardon, being glad to save.

Bitterness.

FROM THE PROSE OF DISRAELI.

MEN weep but once, and then their tears
Contain the bitterness of years.
Bitter it is when first we leave
Our father's hearth, or when, at eve—
After long years in some far land,
By gambling hope's unhappy hand
Returned—we feel a nameless dread,
O'ershadowing change, and kindred dead;
When all the freshness, early loved,
Has been for evermore removed.
Bitter is debt, but bitterer still
Is the accumulated ill,
To be neglected by the good,
Or by beloved ones misconstrued.
Bitter to muse on wasted youth,
Or an exposure of untruth.
Bitter is faith when first beguiled,
Bitter to lose an only child.

Bitter to find no friend to feel,
Or weep in woe, or laugh in weal.
Bitter old age without respect;
The east wind of a child's neglect.
Bitter as death is the untruth
Of one we idolized in youth;
But more embittering than all,
Grief's most unmitigated gall,
Mingles her cup whose marriage proves
The consort of a drunkard's loves:
A hopeless life, delight delayed,
Ambition crushed, belief betrayed.
Love loving still with that fond thirst
Which follows kindness when accursed.
O bitterness beyond compare—
The secret woe which none can share.
Intense as passion half denied,
Deprived of all it deified.
Then rest is torture which denies
Sleep's death of woe to dreaming eyes.
Then night assumes a tardy stay,
And autumn swiftly follows May;
Then first she feels the nothingness
Of *self*, and all that *was*, or *is*.
Then woe could weep on *any* breast,
Since faith is shaken in the *best*.
Then first love's fond delusions die,
And life is left a living lie ;
Yet smiles deceitful o'er distress
As wormwood blooms in bitterness—
A dreadful feeling, cruel, cold,
When youth in all save years is old,
And taunting doubts, a dreary crew
Cry, who is constant, what is true
Among the hopes which move away,
Into the realms of yesterday ?

A Snow Storm at night.

(Near the "Mountain View House," Hamilton.)

To Harry Burkholder, B. A.

NOW winter hovers o'er the hill;
  And coldness into crystal stone
Hath hushed the music of the rill:
  From every bough the birds have flown.

Against the rocks the drifts are driven,
  And storms and winds obstruct the way:
Dark clouds obscure the scowling heaven,
  And frown upon departing day.

Far off and dim the city lights
  Fade faintly through the striving storm;
Like hope which beckons from the heights,
  And leaves the lonely heart to harm.

O for some power to break away
  From this repulsive sullen scene!
So changed from childhood's sunny day,
  From hope, and that which might have been.

Abridge thy dreary future, Time!
  Or give us what we do not gain;
The heart is hardened into crime
  By long accumulated pain.

Yet, source of nature, source of storms,
  Of all that was or is to come,
Let us, before thine awful forms
  Of trouble, be resigned and dumb.

October.

To MAGGIE ZIMMERMAN.

THE winds are high, the forests sigh,
   Dark rolling storms are stern and sable,
The withered weeds and corn-stalks dry
   Sway by the ancient cottage gable.

The black crow on the blighted pine,
   Calls boldly to the flocks high flying:
The world seems restless, and a sign
   Of dimness tells us time is dying.

Far up, the blue Canadian crane
   Slow sails thro' evening's crimson curtain,
He seeks the shady swales again,
   When moonlight makes the shores uncertain.

Among the dark green orchard grass,
   The sanguine sumac boughs are swinging,
The flowers are dead, and dirges pass
   From branch to branch where leaves are clinging.

How wonderful, and dim, and drear,
   Yet beautiful is all around us;
We call for joys that won't appear,
   And mourn the echos that confound us.

Well, well, 'tis better—if we knew
   One half we are so fierce for knowing,
Our world would lose its loveliest hue,
   And Cupid quit his arrow throwing.

Let mercy's mystery mutely pall
   The future's coffined corpses thickly;
If from our eyes the film should fall,
   O, close the cruel curtain quickly.

On Receiving a Piece of Wedding Cake.

ONCE I did scarcely deem that thou
  Wouldst have to *send* this slice so far:
The crust looks luscious, but, somehow
  I have no appetite to share.

A gold-rimmed wrapper and contents,
  Tied with a piece of silken twine,
"Mr. and Mrs.' compliments,"
  And this is all that may be mine.

No need to tell me how the bride
  "Looked lovely dressed in mauve and white;"
I learned that wandering by her side,
  And won her in the pale moonlight.

'Tis said they travel on a tour
  Until the honey-moon's away—
O well, I wish them joy I'm sure!
  We all must journey far some day.

Here is a ring, a wreath, a rose,
  And some fond verses with them given—
O the sweet song!—I wished my foes,
  When first I heard it, all in heaven.

Be still my heart, a piece of cake,
  Enclosed in gold-edged rosy paper,
Should not, in common reason, shake
  Thy pulse to such a silly caper.

Old Stephen.

A DIRGE.

I am dying, Egypt, dying.—SHAKESPEARE.

LET labor lay by till we sing of old Stephen,
  A song he deserves and a spell at the muse;
The faults of his life may you never believe in,
  Nor his who recounts them—but do as you choose.

Old Stephen believed it was wrong to be sober—
  Alas! 'tis the creed of too many we know—
His heart was not hard like the clod in October,
  He often got high to keep memory low.

I knew of his orchard—wherein, a mere urchin,
  I often delayed with my satchel until
The school-master taught me the weight of his birch, in
  The school-house that stood by the tree on the hill.

That school, where I dreaded to go as to prison,
  With tasks still unlearned when the bell did recall
Our steps to the class, and the taws and the lesson:
  Some picture maps hung on the pencil-marked wall.

Tho' fame like an eagle o'er lofty Ben Lomond,
  (A thing quite unlikely) in future should rise,
I'll mind where I carved his young daughter's cognomen
  Beneath the blue light of her beautiful eyes.

His portrait resembled the picture of Pluto,
  Which hung by the door of my grandfather's hall;
His head was an orange tinge, countenance ditto,
  But good was the heart that beat under it all.

So peaceful was he that you could not excite him,
  So learned, that starvation oft stood at his door;
So honest, that all men delighted to cheat him;
  The consequence was, he died perfectly poor.

In the desolate bone-yard they buried his body—
  The spirit had left it some evenings before;
He died in his rocking-chair, sipping hot toddy:
  The toddy got spilled on the dining-room floor.

No more will the dinner-horn call him to supper,
  No more will the barn floor resound to his flail,
No more ride his horse with a grist to the hopper,
  Nor tend to the sugar-bush over the swale.

Regret is not great for the loss of the lowly:
  The poor are expected to give up their breath:
He paid unto nature the debt of his folly,
  And took a receipt from the angel of death.

Yet fate makes us ponder, for once he was pure;
  His childhood, dear reader, was cherished like thine:
We all can sail down Immorality's sewer,
  Or sing with the seraphs forever divine.

◄═══❈═══►

To a Bard.

The glory and the nothing of a name.—BYRON.

THOUGH thou wert born obscurely low,
  And pride keeps down the cry of woe:
Though from the lips of keen distress
Didst thou receive thy natal kiss:
Yea, though thou dwellest where pains prevail,
With bitter stint and sordid bale,
Not in such scenes of solace shorn,
Was thine immortal being born.

Thou too couldst sell thy soul, and be
By slavery from pain set free;
But not for fame dost thou endure
The slight of those who are not pure;
For thou canst scorn the costliest thrones
Where servile slavery grieves and groans.

In Liberty's exultant flight
  'Tis thine to soar celestially,
Through fertile firmaments of light,
  Heaven's sacred scenery to see.

The muse a holy mansion stands,
Upbuilded by Almighty bands,
  O'er Hell's eterne antipodes—
A beacon light its beams have been
  To all who sail life's sullen seas.
Does not the glory of the east
O'er-canopy a costlier feast
Than ever screened a crowned king
In Folly's foul administering ?

The beauty of a thousand worlds,
And every point of light that purls
Eternal boundlessness of space,
Lit with illimitable grace,
With music came that crimson morn,
When this terrestrial globe was born;
And, since thy soul outlasts this earth,
Perchance they chanted at its birth:
Be this thy inspiration's wing,
And thus unto thy spirit sing:

As thou wouldst live hereafter, live !
Give whate'er thou hast to give;
When ruin round thy brethren raves,
Aid them o'er the adverse waves.

If I have chanted what is wrong,
Or woven folly with my song,
Or caused one kindred human heart
From what it loves to keep apart,
Then shake from out thy glass, O Time,
Oblivion's ashes on my rhyme.

⟨⟶✦⟵⟩

To Alexander Goforth.

THE spring returns; by the old mill
   Forth issues the rejoicing rill.
The birds are here, and every tree
Is robed in green to greet their glee,
Midst soft warm vapors, early showers,
Red-glinting dews, and blushing flowers—
I wish their innocence were ours.
How beautiful is earth!—O you
Who bid us scorn it, teach untrue.
'Tis human sin that clouds our sky,
"And drags or drives us on to die:"
'Tis crime's infernal flag unfurled
Which sheds such shadows round our world;
Making life's path a thorny glade,
Crooked as falsehood when afraid.
'Tis self-wrought wrong which makes us mourn,
And mars whatever might adorn
The little left us here to bless
The human heart with happiness:
And every implement of ill
Seems hurled against an upward will;
   For death is in the world, and all
      Its happiest spirits sigh
   The delicate, the beautiful,
      However dear, must die.
   The fruitful trees in bloom arrayed,
      In vales of vivid green,
   Fleck with manœuvring light and shade
      The grave of what has been.

———— ◦ ◦ ————

The Growth of What is Excellent is Slow.

————

So slow
The growth of what is excellent; so hard
To attain perfection in this nether world.—COWPER.

————

MILLIONS of cycles must have passed, preparing
  The world, e'er Eden's gorgeous garden bloomed ;.
Thousands have fall'n, Galileo-like, for daring
. To teach men truth, by heavenly light illumed.
The best have not succeeded best, but perished,
  Like brands hurled out upon the wintry snow;
And thousands more will fall who should be cherished, ·
  For the growth of what is excellent is slow.

Regretted joys, lost years, a future darkened,   •
  These are the phases of our destiny:
The holiest hopes to which our hearts have hearkened,
  Like fairest flowers, are first to fade away.
The gladdest hours of life oft deeply grieve us,
  And leave most pain, we know not why; but know
That those we put most faith in first deceive us,
  For the growth of what is excellent is slow.

Yet be not baffled, thou who hast the yearning
  For that which is essentially divine!
Be not discouraged at the slow returning
  Of all thine earnest efforts, nor repine.
The talent God has given thee is strengthened
  While battling with adversity, although
The distance from thine object may seem lengthened,
  For the growth of what is excellent is slow.

  5

Remember 'tis at night the stars are shining;
  In rugged regions richest fruitage thrives;
The furnace of affliction is refining;
  And double talent is his share who strives.
Among life's roses thorns are thickly blended;
  And in the tempest only shines the bow—
Even while the shades are far o'er fate extended;
  For the growth of what is excellent is slow.

Swine.

The full-fed swine return with evening home.—HOMER.

BEHOLD the hog! who has not heard the praise
  Of all the birds that sing, or beasts that graze?
Yet, strange neglect, we seldom hear a word
In praise of pork or bacon, ham or lard.
Why should we show so much ingratitude,
To those whose flesh is universal food?
Is this an ancient grudge remembered still,
'Gainst Satan's refuge running down the hill?
Why blame the modern hog for sins extinct?
Save in a few to our own species linked,—
Some perpendicular porkers, men in shape,
Who meanly sneak in every office gap—
Nerve-bent on gain—the power of grasping more—
With ceaseless toil "till life's poor play is o'er."

But truth will triumph, and it ever should,
As pounded glass will sparkle though in mud.
The hog shall have his due.   Come, lofty muse,
Grant them the fame their fates so long refuse.
Come, sprightly visions, retribution come,
All things that sigh in song or blush in bloom.

The bull-frog croaking in the deep milldam,
Whose smothered thunders break the evening calm,
The cowbell tinkling in the twilight shade,
The airy tinting on the landscape laid,
The golden fruit upon the green sward spread,
From fertile boughs, by fragrant breezes shed,
The perfumed air, the rose cloud high and still,
The stream-bound vale, the lonely whip-poor-will,
Whose vespers vibrate down the vested aisles—
Where parting day on pensive evening smiles:
Ye, shades and shapes of slighted swine, appear!
Each with your knife-docked tail, or half-slit ear,
Slow sauntering down the lane, with muddy heels,
To snuff frankincense from the buckwheat fields:
Or carrying straw before an autumn storm,
To keep thy cozy slumbering places warm ;
Or grunting restless round steep stacks of straw,
When chilly winds are easterly and raw ;
Come and confute your foes, force them to see
Who is the most to blame, themselves or thee.
Appeal to reason, and if none remains,
Appeal to appetite ! there all have brains.

They come ! they come ! ye gourmands raise your eyes,
See double rows of sausages arise !
From ham and eggs the soothing steam comes wavy—
From mashed potatoes waiting for the gravy.
Sweet saliva-exciting elixir,
'Tis thine to make the hungry stomach stir.
Then comes the dough-nuts—boys can best divulge
How Santa Claus makes the new sock-heels bulge.

Great commerce, scorning paltry views of caste,
Floats bacon loads along the watery waste:
To dicker with for what is needed home,
Or to supply the sailors as they roam
By far off isles, in oriental seas,
Where spices waft unfailing fragrancies,

(O fields, green fields, the fields of orient spring,
Where crimson birds all day and insects sing);
Laden with silks her ships recross the main,
And sighing damsels learn to smile again.

'Tis said, and truly, that our food contains
The various properties of various brains.
Byron called bacon amatory food;
Hence its great influence for bad or good.
However this may be, one fact is sure,
That to the good and pure all things are pure.

Some hide-bound blunderers of a purblind school,
Who think th' omniverous animal, man, a fool,
Maintain the blest millennium soon would greet
This purse-mad world, if man did eat no meat;
That earth would be quick purged from all distress,
And brotherly love come by the first express.

'Tis not in eating part, or eating all,
Will purify our morals, heart or gall.
How meat makes mind no mortal known can tell;
And since we in such stupid ignorance dwell,
E'en let it rest with our uncertain sins,
Till proved where pork-mind ends or beef's begins.
For almost any creed a man can choose,
Will leave his mind one-sided in its views,
Especially when judging the unblest,
Who sin outside the sect which he thinks best.

No universal rule will suit all cases,
Our stomachs differ, as our fates or faces.
A moderate use of all things under heaven
Is the best precept that the learned have given.
One worthy truth life teaches every hour,
That temperance gives us health, and health gives power.
Not so the dram, one universal curse
Sends its partakers to the hopeless hearse.
We leave the argument on reason's shelf—
Let every stomach civilize itself.

But Mr. Bull, Lord John, would suffer most
Keenly, deprived of his diurnal roast.
One beefless week would fade Great Britain's bloom,
And probably blacken history years to come.
Their warriors could not fight, nor sailors sail;—
All their internal mechanism fail;—
But give them beef, half-cooked, and I engage
Lord J. will fold his arms and smile at Fenian rage.

In every possible clime where food is found,
Do hungry swine-herds graze or root the ground.
By bowery banyan trees, or towery palms,
Persistently he cultivates his hams:
As persevering and prolific still
As Scotia's sons, thriving in good or ill.

But when the season wanes into the fall,
Then comes the saddest, bloodiest sight of all!
The big fat barrow, in his sty of straw,
Must die—'tis life's inevitable law.
The long knife lets the life-blood from his breast,
Or the quick rifle gives his spirit rest.
Sad fate, but certain; let him rest in peace;
And let the big boys sop his bacon grease.
Hale lads hard laboring, in the autumn air,
Require a huge amount of healthy fare;
Else they will sally forth, beneath the moon,
To roast the corn or slay the sly racoon.

Now the same pots that stewed his nibs of corn,
His pea and pumpkin provender at morn,
Contain a boiling flood to scald his hair,
Ere from the scaffold hangs his bacon bare.
No more for him to root the flowery mead,
Or come with upcurled narrative to feed;
No more to stand the barn-yard bars outside,
Squealing for entrance at the eventide.

No more to husk the yellow corn for him,
In fine October, when the days are dim
Yet beautiful in haziness, and still,
Yea happy as a hungry swine at swill.

Who has not seen on Indian summer days
A youthful party husking yellow maize?
.When crimson Autumn comes with copious horn
To crown the furrows with abundant corn,
When restless Sol rolls eastern night away,
And pearly dews gleam in the early day;
Only such clouds as torrid heats restrain,
Move their vast glory o'er the gaudy plain;
When thistle beards triumphant ride the breeze,
And golden sunbeams kindle golden trees;
When purpling clusters, as the winds abound,
Trail their long tendrils o'er the dark green ground.
Then rosy romping girls and boys agree
To help each other at the husking bee.
There laughter too comes, "holding both his sides;"
Frequently thence are chosen future brides.
From the choice band up wakes the general cheer,
As blushing beauty finds the ruby ear.
As her white hands disrobe the gracious grain,
None but her bosom knows her tender pain.
Her tingling cheeks, suffused, alone would prove
The crimson symbol prophesying love.
Yet sly refusing that he should redeem
The forfeit pledge, with many a modest scream—
Pretended poutings over stolen kisses
From make-believe-resisting ready misses—
O early gladness! by whatever name
We call thee, thou art holier than fame;
Or all the joys that visit us in vain,
Among the passing years of hardening pain.

The Little Frame House at the foot of the Hill.

HOW often there comes to the spirit, when lonely,
　　Some picture of beauty to gladden our toil:
Some rose of wrecked prospects left blossoming only,
　　In thistles and thorns of adversity's soil.
And fadelessly fancy retains the reflection,
　　As rocks that are rolled in the midst of a rill,
Yet few things can equal in sweet recollection
　　The little frame house at the foot of the hill.

A meadow of green has a stream running through it,
　　Where speckled fish sport, and the birds sing their song
In groves whose red branches at autumn bestrew it,
　　And fleck the blue waters that wander along.
But 'tis not all these that most beauty abides in,
　　It is not the mead with its flowery rill
That sweetens remembrance, but she who resides in
　　The little frame house at the foot of the hill.

Her song is as sweet as the song of the robin
　　That sings by the stream, on the still summer eve;
Her heart is the purest that ever did throb in
　　A beautiful breast, for the love it relieves;
Her words are the kindest that ever connected
　　Two fates with that magical sentence, I will:
No wonder my heart for its Mecca selected
　　The little frame house at the foot of the hill.

O Sol, shed the glow of thy beautiful glory!
　　Rise mornings of light, and beam evenings of peace;
Come flowers with music to make her life's story
　　A heart full of love, every day to increase.
Let him, the one choice of her soul, be unswerving
　　In that which gives life its most exquisite thrill:
Sweet destinies fail not in kindly observing
　　The little frame house at the foot of the hill.

The Old Number Four Plough.

LAST time I returned to my father's plantation,
  The light of the landscape was vividly green:
The breezes were full of the sweet exhalation
  Of flowers and song, and the sky was serene.
My spirit rejoiced in the beauty of summer,
  And fancy took flights unattempted before;
But suddenly sank when I saw a new-comer
  Had taken the place of the Old Number Four.

My joy was dispelled by the shadows of sorrow,
  As all the reverses arose into view,
Since guiding that plough with its share like an arrow,
  Its iron-bound beam, and its handles of blue.
For oft in the fields, when the crimson of morning
  Made golden the mists on night's shadowy shore,
When wood-robins welcomed the daylight returning,
  I followed the furrow with Old Number Four;

And all the day blest with the thrilling reflection
  That soon as the eventide slowly drew near,
By chance I would meet with the blushing perfection
  Of golden-haired Anna, the tenderly dear;
And wander with her, in the glory a sharer,
  'Neath roseate skies round June's flowery floor,
Till earth seemed to fade and the heavens come nearer
  The fields that were furrowed by Old Number Four

Perhaps, after all, 'tis this rose of our spirits
  Plucked out of life's wormwood, yet gathered in vain,
That gives the old plough such a halo of merits,
  Being mingled with joys that return not again ;
My heart fondly looks from life's wearisome changes,
  And beats for the beauty that blest it of yore,
And loves to contemplate, wherever it ranges,
  The rapture connected with Old Number Four.

The Old Pine Canoe.

TO MY BROTHER.

YOU remember the days that have long ago faded
  From hills that stand high in the sun's breezy beams;
The flower-spangled shore by the cedar tree shaded,
  And the bridge where we fished in the many-curved streams.
You remember the boat turned all gray by the weather,
  That often we sailed into where the grapes grew:
We climbed to the tops of the tall vines together,
  And watched the waves cradle the old pine canoe.

But where is the glory ambition projected,
  When gaily we roved o'er the water-bound scene?
Where now is the gladness that bright scene reflected,
  Ah, where is the boat that we moored on the green?
The spirit of change has all silently taken
  The charm that we loved from the objects we knew:
The beauty has fled, and our friends have forsaken
  The scenes where we paddled the old pine canoe.

Never again will they come to rejoice us,
  When evening's first sunbeams repose on the hill:
Never again will we hear their glad voices,
  Save when the loved echoes of memory thrill.
If we gather once more those the grave has not gathered,
  To join in the joys we were wont to pursue,
We could not forget all the sorrows that withered
  The days since we sailed in the old pine canoe.

Farewell to the fair waving valley forever,
  Farewell to the flowers that grew by the shore,
Farewell to the course of the blue winding river,
  Farewell to the scenes that can gladden no more!
The spring will return, and the season of roses ;
  The forest and valleys their verdure renew,
But the friends of those scenes that our memory shows us,
  Have past down time's stream like the old pine canoe.

5*

'Tis better not to know.

(R. R. DONNELLEY.)

WHO ever formed great plans in youth,
　　Of mighty things to do,
Of wisdom, fortune, fame and power,
　　To aid the good and true?
Who ever wished to bless his race,
　　To raise the poor and low?
Such patriot hearts have felt some pains,
　　'Tis better not to know.

Has bright temptation lured thee on
　　To its fair gleaming goal,
Till harsh remorse to greater sins
　　Goads on thy harrowed soul?
Hopes wrecked by rocks along life's stream
　　For evermore laid low,
There are some moments in such scenes
　　'Tis better not to know.

We plod all feebly on through fate,
　　Dumb, wretched, tempted, blind:
Forbid to hope, and by remorse
　　Forbid to look behind.
Resigned to the uncertainty
　　Of everything but woe;
With doubts forboding future pain,
　　'Tis better not to know.

Tumultuous passions surge the soul,
　　And fitful visions flash—
Grief-chilled, and fever-scorched by turns,
　　'Neath pain's all-torturing lash.
Desiring death, if but for change;
　　Yet dreading hence to go;
For in that sleep what dreams may come,
　　'Tis better not to know.

For in that dim futurity—
   All hazy lone and far—
Upon whose threshold Silence sits,
   And holds death's door ajar
For souls to enter at all hours,
   While from his house none go,
There may be secrets hidden there
   'Tis better not to know.

The longing after hidden lore,
   The thirst for unknown things,
The fearful yearnings to explore
   The future's mystic springs;
The blighted happiness, and all,
   All that we must forego,
Through want of wisdom's light, perchance
   'Tis better not to know.

But wisdom makes us worthy heaven,
   And knowledge gives us power ;
And holy science floods the soul,
   As with a golden shower ;
And nature's studies speak of Him
   From whom they brightly flow ;
Whose lightest joy outweighs those cares
   'Tis better not to know.

Then let us fathom every truth
   'Tis possible to find ;
To strengthen, bless and beautify
   Man's truth-desiring mind ;
Earth's lights and shades, and all the stars
   That soul-exalting glow,
Can teach to bear the numerous ills
   'Tis better not to know.

November.—A Dirge.

THE old oak tree is dying;
  The storm-tanned branch of centuries is bare;
The bark is riven from the trunk and lying
    Distant and near:
The last fair robe of summer leaves is flying,
    Withered and sear.

    Departing wild birds gather,
On the high branches, ere they haste away;
Singing their farewell to the frigid ether,
    And fading day:
To sport no more o'er withered mead or heather,
    No longer gay.

    And sullenly assuming
His throne, to vindicate the summer past,
Stern autumn stops the thunder's distant booming,
    And lighthing's blast,
While from the north the dreary clouds are coming,
    Sombre and vast.

    The little cricket's singing
Sounds lonely in the crisp and yellow leaves,
Like by-gone tones of tenderness, up-bringing
    A thought that grieves—
A bell upon a ruined turret ringing
    On Sabbath eves.

    The tempest-loving raven,
Pilot of storms across the silent sky,
Soars loftily along the heaving heaven,
    With doleful cry,
Ut'ring lone dirges—thistle-beards are driven
    Where the winds sigh.

And yet here is a flower,
Still lingering, by the changing season spared!
And a lone bird within a leafless bower—
Two friends who dared
To share the shadows of misfortune's hour,
Though unprepared.

<hr/>

Song.

THE WARM-HEARTED GRASP OF A WORKING MAN'S HAND.

IN changes and partings 'tis pleasant to find
The friends we most value still constant and kind:
Oh! sweet the reception that beauty can give,
With the soul-thrilling pressure that bids hope to live;
But the noblest reception that nature has planned,
Is the warm-hearted grasp of a working man's hand.

There is beauty in light, as the rainbow can prove;
There is glory in labor, and rapture in love:
There is valor in peace, and experience in years;
There is power in joy, and a magic in tears;
There is greatness in toil that too few understand,
And the warm-hearted grasp of a working man's hand.

How piteous that those who do labor's least share,
Are caressed by earth's fools, and preferred by the fair:
And life after life is to vanity wrecked,
That reason would save if allowed to reflect;
But the holiest alliance by love ever fanned
Is the warm-hearted grasp of a working man's hand.

Burns.

ALL hail to the birth-day that dawned on thy being!
   A nation's best gift blessed her bosom that morn:
The generous glow of thy genius far-seeing,
   Of nobleness, boldness, and manliness born.

The cloud of adversity gathered around thee,
   And fortune seemed pinioned by poverty's chain,
Their Hinnom-like hopelessness failed to confound thee;
   All chains for thy spirit were welded in vain.

Though cramped by obscurity's low occupation,
   ·It seemed but to quicken thine intellect strong:
It served but to make thee the earth's admiration,
   The glory and boast of a nation of song.

By the lofty Ben Lomond, in ether projecting
   His cavernous crags, where the cold breezes moan;
By the beautiful Ayr, in its bosom reflecting
   The sun, moon and stars, as they shine or have shone;

Thy genius was quickened, sublimely reposing
   Where fancies ecstatic at evening arise—
From grandeur and beauty, to mortals disclosing
   Celestial reflections and heavenly dyes.

Bequeathing mankind what no time or detraction,
   Or truth-testing changes can ever destroy—
A soul-soothing essence, a balm for dejection,
   A tender assurance of innocent joy.

Thy songs have a power to strengthen the spirit,
   To dissipate gloom in life's desolate hours:
What doubles the rapture of Cupid's quick merit
   Like the might of thy music's most mystical powers?

On the altar of Beauty exhaustless devotion
   Outpouring in favour of virtue and love!
All eloquent teachings of tender emotion:
   How hard is the heart that thy tones cannot move!

For the strength of thy soul seized the subjects around thee,
   And made thy creations posterity's praise;
Till the nations who gaze would rejoice to have crowned thee
   With the palm branch of peace and the laurel's green bays.

The might of thy passionate mind could not slumber,
   But soared in the scenes of delight and despair:
Enwrapped in the rapture of hope's happy number,
   Or wandering oppressed on the banks of the Ayr.

How often those dreams that delight in the distance
   Are woefully marred, when adversity's force
Stops the feeling's fond flow, with a sullen resistance,
   Like the stream's wave rolled back by the storm from its
                             [course!

Yet it seemed of thy nature to gild life with glory,
   With fancy to fashion what was not to be:
Uphoarding each hope and encouraging story,
   That painted a future from misery free.

Light of the days that are ours no longer,
   Remnant of rapture departed for aye,
Still grows the strength of thine influence stronger,
   Gathering power as years pass away.

Time cannot extinguish the light of thy genius,
   By nature conferred to ennoble mankind:
An antidote sent to exalt and to wean us
   From folly's allurements that trammel the mind.

In the "Temple of Fame" the great Fergusson slumbers,
   Where Campbell recorded a praiseworthy name,
Where Cherubims chant æsthetical numbers:
   But whose fame can equal the light of thy fame

September.

ONCE more the maple leaves begin to strew
    The walks and streams:
There is a sadness in their transient hue,
    Like twilight's beams—
Rich as the tintings fancy loves to view,
    In life's fond dreams.

We knew that June's green hues from hill and glade
    Would disappear;
But ah, we did not think their time to fade
    Already here—
Behold, the trees are brilliantly arrayed
    In Autumn's sere!

And every June seems shorter in its stay,
    With all its pride!
Before the morning dew has passed away
    'Tis eventide:
We watch the flowers appear—another day,
    And they have died.

So pass we, one by one, health flushed, hope fired,
    In manhood's prime,
At any hour by desolate Death required,
    In his dim clime:
Millions of figures, transiently attired,
    Marching through time.

We missed the roses' fragrace from the air,
    When in our walks;
We sought them where they grew but found naught there,
    Save some lone stalks,
Some bright blue flowerets, and a scanty share
    Of hollyhocks.

Dark clouds arrange their shadows round the hill:
    On every gale
Leaps forth the yellow leaves—the whip-poor-will
    Has left the vale:
Long sable clouds of black-birds, singing shrill,
    Slow southward sail.

The awful majesty of storms will come
    And blight the green!
And all the grand array of summer bloom
    Be no more seen:
Each day contains the universal doom
    Of what has been.

❧

The Comet.

I TRAVEL a road to a farther abode
  Than thy wondering thoughts can wander:
My career in the sky is so ample and high,
  The heavens intervening roll under.
The width of my sphere encompass each year,
  And cycle of time rolled together:
I gleam in the light of my musical flight,
  O'er realms of eternity's ether.

O'er stars that were made when Jehovah arrayed
  Creation's first dawning with fire;
O'er each orbit and earth, thy Creator launched forth,
  Through heaven that morning, and prior.
O'er amethyst thrones and the star-spangled zones
  Of the Ruler of regions sublime;
O'er forests and streams in the beautiful beams,
  Which come from the color of time.

'Tis piteous to see what a little to thee
  Makes greatness, and troubles thy reason,
In thy trebly cursed world which Jehovah hath hurled,
  His footstool in space for a season.

Thy low superstitions, thy vaulting ambitions,
    The wiles of the learned who have shammed,
Mingling lies with their lore, until ignorance and war
    Have peopled the realms of the damned.

Man's pride of an hour grows despotic in power,
    Uprearing vast temples to sin,
Till Reason and Right, in their beautiful light,
    Stand trembling but enter not in.
The excellent few who would teach what is true,
    Have portions peculiarly hard:
The day will arrive when their wishes shall thrive,
    With peaceful, abundant reward.

I'll bring thee a grace from the splendors of space,
    A beam from the beauty of heaven;
Then earth will assume such unlimited bloom
    As angels of Paradise live in.
'Tis part of my mission to allume earth's condition,
    To silence the wail of Death's story;   —
There's many a sphere in my spacious career,
    Has grown out of gloom into glory.

There cometh a light to enkindle thy night,
    To dissipate grovelling fear:
So sang they that morn when thy birth-place was born,
    With harps of each limitless sphere:
With harps that were given the angels in heaven,
    When Eden's first Sabbath shone clear:
These anthems that roll for the seraphim soul,
    Would madden a mortal to hear.

Thou wilt bathe in an orb that will wholly absorb
    The shade that is ruled by the moon:
In light that surrounds will burst forth the grand sounds
    Of heaven's whole concert in tune:
The just shall be filled with such glory as thrilled
    The happy, in heaven that be:
The lightning prongs of their suffering wrongs
    Shall smile like a sunrise at sea.

Intemperance.

MOST human evils warn us ere they come,
But wine can render all objections dumb.
As when a wanderer in an unknown land,
Leaves the right road for one by pleasure planu'd,
How bright the flowers appear! the trees, how fair:
All joys, long sought for, seem to flourish there;
Where purpling clusters, when the winds abound,
Trail their long tendrils o'er the dark green ground.
Lo, any man whose spirit longs for light,
May enter there, those vistas are so bright;
But soon, how soon! the cheerful scene is changed;
Zig-zag the road through thorns and brambles ranged;
Neglected guide-boards sink into the sand,
While barren deserts burn the blasted land:
Such fearful ruins hide his former way,
No human knows how far he is astray.
So when the soul leaves duty's dreary beat,
For bacchanal delights and dalliance sweet,
The mind for once seems full of pleasant things,
And the soul revels in the realm of kings.
With each red draught the veins their youth renew,
And fancies all the fields of space review.
O ye who say, "Wine brings us but despair,"
Know not the dreadful fascinations there.
'Tis this that blinds the reason, blasts the sense,
And shuts the right hand of Omnipotence;
This cheers the dreary drunkard's downward path,
This cheats his soul of all save woe and death;
For sure re-action comes; the nerves outworn,
Fiercely rebellious, natural blessings scorn.
Then where those scenes supernal? here but now;
And thou, O queenly pleasure, where art thou?
Thy transport turned to torture, thy delight
To degradation turned, thy bloom to blight;
Regret and shame like vultures haunt the scene,
And hinnoms of despair o'er what has been;

There gamblers nurse their guilty hopes of gain ;
Red suicide is there, and the insane.
Spirits immortal steeped in secret shame,
And foul disease that has not any name.

It *must* be in the annals of mankind,
That we are born to our best interest blind ;
The moral sight, long fixed on themes untrue,
Must lose the sense of right which once it knew,
Else how could christians, sacred from offence,
Rest till this plague-spot had departed hence.
Could we but look upon this curse aright,
Mercy would hinder sleep until the blight
Were wholly banished soon.   O men of worth,
Why art thou mute ?   Why art thou mute, O earth ?
The unabortive beast, the stones might rise,
Rebuking human inconsistencies.

When mad O'Neil, with his unholy host,
Approached for spoils upon our glorious coast,
The sons of those who bled for peace before,
Rose to a man and drove them from our shore.
The stalwart offspring of the sturdy race
Of Britons could not brook the great disgrace,
But in our midst a foe—by patriots nursed—
A foe insidious works, of all, the worst,
(The direst enemies are those within,
Yet sects, who fight on faith, assist this sin.)
By commerce nurtured, for the sake of gain,
By Legislation sanctioned, to profane.

We build expensive jails for the undone,
Yet leave the cause of all their crimes alone.
We grudge our tax, while silently consume
Whole holocusts of a continual hecatomb.
Across our land it sweeps like a simoon,
And thousands revel darkly to their doom.
Yea, thousands yearly reel along the path,
The self-same road their fathers took to death ;
From the proud palace, from the reeking cell,
From gin-holes, from abodes respectable,

From learning's halls, from " wisdom's way " they rove,
From holy hopes, and from the arms of love.
Alas, how must a mother's bosom bleed,—
Her best years gone—when sons no warnings heed!
The shrines on which to rest her patient brow,
Like broken reeds—self-reeling to and fro.

O wrinkled mothers—prematurely gray !
O sisters, and those dearer far than they !
Alas for thine affections, which *will* rise,
And prove thee kindred to the waiting skies.
Alas for thy fond heart, so prone to break,
In silence o'er the miseries we make.

Ye who first guide the young, the ungrown host—
Surely they want our help and warning most !
Wake each warm conscience on this fatal theme,
Before they launch on the alluring stream.

'Tis sad that we, ere life is well begun—
How brief the stay ! how apt to be undone !
Knowing that life's short lease is insecure,
Knowing we must immortally endure—
That we those high prerogatives of gain,
Exchange for earthly husks, and future pain ;
Exchange for dregs, a heritage on high,
And day by day deliberately die.

What must the angels think of us, and thou,
O sin-slain Son of God ! with Thy sacred brow,
Thy purple hands outstretched to win and woo,
With all our sins Thy spirit pierced anew—
A sacrifice which does not seem to stay
The fearful fullness of our infamy,
And yet such power has evil, that we know
The soul to be immortal by its woe.

A Letter

Found in the street, supposed to be written by one of the Officer's Married Widows to another, on the removal of the 69th.

I answer as soon as I am able :
 After our terrible loss,
My nerves are exceeding unstable ;
 My husband complains I am cross ;
But fate has so coldly bereft us,
 No motive remains to improve,
Alas ! since the Officers left us,
 With only our husbands to love.

You need not curtail your confession :
 Let sympathy solace your pain ;
I often repeat your expression :
 " We met a great loss in those men."
Ah me ! if we never had known them
 We might have endured the old groove,
But now to fall back on our own men,
 With only our husbands to love !

Those ladies who came to me (calling
 On purpose to watch and to blame)
I nearly was fainting and falling,
 So coldly they uttered his name !
I never could blame any woman
 For letting her sentiments rove ;
O ! life is a task super-human,
 With only one's husband to love.

It might have been borne if they never
 Had jingled their swords on our street ;
But only to taste, then forever,
 Forego the ambrosial treat ;
For who can replenish the pleasure
 We lost on their sudden remove ?
No nectar remains in life's measure,
 With only a husband to love.

How mean are the ways of civilians,
 Compared to war's wonderful trade !
Those officers dissipate millions,
 And are not of spending afraid.
The worst of their lot is, like seamen,
 It constantly calls them to move,
And thus they make widows of women
 With only a husband to love.

The husband I married acts kindly,
  He keeps every vow that he swore,
But wakes not my spirit so blindly
  As one I intensely adore.
That one wears his buskins so sweetly!
  He moves as a monarch should move!
O, life has departed completely,
  With only our husbands to love!

Our children! we love them all dearly;
  But, wherefore deny the stern truth?
Their startling developments yearly,
  Increase our long distance from youth.
Let nature those pledges present us,
  Outnumbering the leaves in the grove,
Such troubles would fail to torment us
  Like only a husband to love.

The last time I met my Apollo,
  How lovely the valley, how green!
I wish every word I could follow
  With which he transfigured *that scene*.
My husband is pious and prosy,
  Too tame are his fancies to rove;
My midnights are dreary and dozy,
  With only a husband to love.

They say 'tis immoral to mingle
  My thoughts with another man's fate;
But often the soul remains single,
  When bodies connubial mate.
He argues, and proves it with reason,
  He calls up my feelings to prove,
" Fine wives with dull men make it treason
  With only one husband to love."

He says that my nature is tender,
  He says that my form is refined,
He says that my bust is so slender,
  He says that my husband is blind;
He says that our laws are a blunder,
  He says our delights they reprove,
He says I 'm unblest, and no wonder:
  With only one husband to love.

P. S. I will write to him often,
  His letters relieve my long stay,
Their sacred communings can soften,
  The fate which has forced him away.
May be I can make some excuses
  To meet him at London, by Jove,
We women have plenty of ruses,
  With only one husband to love.

Opinions of the Press

ON THE AUTHOR'S PREVIOUS PUBLICATIONS.

From Mrs. Susanna Moodie.

Your book may take its stand upon the same shelf with McQueen, McLauchlin and Sangster (men of undoubted genius, who have done much to enrich the literature of this country), and lose nothing by the comparison.

From Rev. W. Ormiston, D. D.

"The Canadian Lyre," a small volume of poems, by J. R. Ramsay, a young bard of great powers and promise. In style, simple and chaste; in versification, smooth and musical; in imagery, natural and national; in sentiment, pure and elevating—these poems cannot fail at once to please and profit.

I gratefully accept them as an earnest of something still nobler to follow, and cordially commend them to all true lovers of poetry and patriotic patrons of a Canadian literature.

From Rev. Lachlan Taylor.

I have much pleasure in adding my testimony to that which is here presented with so much comprehensiveness.

From Charles Sangster.

A host of similar attempts could be quoted to which it is vastly superior.

From William Wye Smith.

I think it is a happy thing for Canada that we have young men among us who devote this highest of mental gifts—poetry—to the service of their country, for *it is serving* our country, by teaching us to love her, her people and her scenery, as much as though in arms on her behalf. His muse sometimes rises to a height in eloquence which the novice may not hope to attain, as witness the following, where he speaks of hope as a seraph :

> To his own happy occupation singing
> The song begun in Heaven before the life
> The hosts of holy worshipers ;

And again of a scene where—

> The sacred, superhuman hues
> Adorned each dim declivity,
> And shaped the intermingled views
> As fair as Eden's landscapes be.

Had I the public ear at command, I should certainly have a " proclamation poetic " made in your favor.

From the Hamilton " Spectator."

His contributions have invariably been rhythmical and smooth in composition—pure and poetic in sentiment. For instance, here is a beautiful little lilt:

I SHALL NOT TELL.

I shall not tell thee why the land
 With so much gladness glows;
There is but one in all the world
 My sacred secret knows.

O, she is fairer than the flowers
 Of rosy June or May—
When every bird is singing near,
 And every blossom gay.

I asked her eyes to let their beams
 Make life supremely grand;
Their answer, like a flood of light,
 Flushed all the flowery land.

The sunbeams glanced among the grass,
 Warm-waving in the breeze;
A new life gladdened every bloom—
 More vivid grew the trees.

I never had much faith in gain,
 Or wealth of golden power;
Now even these seem doubly vain,
 Henceforward, from this hour.

I shall not tell thee why the land
 With so much glory glows;
There is but one in all the world
 My sacred secret knows.

We must content ourselves for the present, with another quotation :

A SIGH.

'Tis strange whatever makes us blest
 Can mar the bliss it gives,
By planting in the tender breast
 The thorn that never leaves.

'Tis strange, what gives us most delight
 Can its own hope destroy,
And hurl the spirit from the height
 Of its unfinished joy.

Why do our souls, with so much room
 For bliss, yet grieve ? ah ! why
Do joys, like fragile flowers, bloom
 To dazzle and to die ?

From the Hamilton "Banner."

His language is generally bold, eloquent and musical ; he is imaginative and sentimental, and gives evidence of genuine genius. We are glad this volume has been published, as it is certainly a great addition to the meagre literature of this Province.

From the Owen Sound "Times."

The young bard is not afraid to see poetry in the Canadian landscape around him, and we honor him for it.

THE SPINNING WHEEL.

Here is the vale, the elm tree and the oak
  All leave-crowned still!
The old log barn—ah, it was here awoke
  My heart's first thrill :
Here was life's sunniest spot, love's tender tone,
  Hope's bliss made real,
All ruled by one whose slaves were hearts, whose throne
  A spinning wheel.

'Twas on the wheat floor of this same old barn
  One morning, she
Set me to hold a hank of tangled yarn,
  And tangled me :
Yes, it was here the fairy came to spin,
  And I to reel
The long, long thread from love's commingled skein
  Round fate's strange wheel.

All the perfection sixteen Junes could shed
  Was her sweet share :
Soft auburn glories cluster'd round her head—
  Ah, she was fair !
Yet did not seem to know the thread she spun
  With so much zeal
Was the beginning of a finer one
  By that same wheel.

Though I have been afar, my heart will pay
  A reverence still,
E'en to that old neglected barn of grey
  Beside the hill.
And much as misery may interfere
  With human weal,
In memory's pleasing solitudes I hear
  The Spinning Wheel.

From the "Canada Evangelist."

These poems furnish evidence of powers which, under due culture, would not fail of achieving a high place in our country's early literature.

From the New Orleans "True Delta."

There is a breathing of the fragrant meadows in his verses which is quite refreshing to the literary palates of sun-baked city readers.

www.ingramcontent.com/pod-product-compliance
Lightning Source LLC
Chambersburg PA
CBHW030546270326
41927CB00008B/1544